A Case for Case Studies

An Immigrant's Journal

Paul R. Abramson

SAGE PUBLICATIONS
The International Professional Publishers
Newbury Park   London   New Delhi

For information address:

SAGE Publications, Inc.
2455 Teller Road
Newbury Park, California 91320

SAGE Publications Ltd.
6 Bonhill Street
London EC2A 4PU
United Kingdom

SAGE Publications India Pvt. Ltd.
M-32 Market
Greater Kailash I
New Delhi 110 048 India

Printed in the United States of America

Library of Congress Cataloging-in-Publication Data

Abramson, Paul R., 1949-
  A case for case studies: an immigrant's journal / Paul R. Abramson.
    p.   cm.
  Includes bibliographical references.
  ISBN 0-8039-3695-8—ISBN 0-8039-3696-6 (pbk.)
  1. Jews—Byelorussian S.S.R.—Svisloch' (Grodnenskaia oblast')—
Diaries. 2. Svisloch' (Grodnenskaia oblast', Byelorussian S.S.R.)—
Ethnic relations. 3. Immigrants—United States—Diaries. 4. Jews—
United States—Diaries. 5. Sociology—Biographical methods.
I. Title.
DS135.R9S9242 1992   91-16079
947'.65004924—dc20   CIP

FIRST PRINTING, 1992

Sage Production Editor: Judith L. Hunter

CONTENTS

"But in this Discourse I shall be very happy to show the paths I have followed, and to set forth my life as in a picture, so that everyone may judge of it for himself; and thus in learning from the common talk what are the opinions which are held of it, a new means of obtaining self-instruction will be reached, which I shall add to those which I have been in the habit of using."

—René Descartes
Discourse on the Method

PREFACE

This book attempts to make a case for case studies. In doing so, it introduces two simple rationales. First, it suggests that case studies may serve as inductive input, either to elaborate a normative response, or to document an infrequent occurrence. Second, this book also suggests that case studies fall within Karl Popper's definition (and method) of science, if such projects are careful to articulate threats to both internal and external validity.

This book also introduces case study data in the form of a diary, written over a 12-year period by a Russian Jewish immigrant. Prior to introducing the diary, the book furnishes details about the process of translation and preparation. In addition, brief historical material is included to provide perspective to the diary.

Finally, this book has an unusual twist. Although ostensibly it is about social science methodology, it is also about my family. The diaries were written by my grandfather, Samuel Abramson. Thus, this book is a hybrid of sorts, part personal quest, part methodological critique.

To accommodate this strange balancing act I have opted for a simple solution. This book strives for an honest portrayal of the facts, plus a full disclosure of all the inherent biases, within the context of exploring the scientific rationale for case study research. I hope I have surmounted the obvious limitations in this work, so as to make this book a broader contribution to the literature.

In working on this project for the past five years I have profited from many discussions with colleagues. Most notably, I want to thank Dick Berk, Ruth Fisher, and Mac Runyan. Professor Runyan has set the standard for life history research and graciously shared his ideas with me. Similarly, Professor Berk has been a wonderful gadfly—always debating statistical and methodological issues. And finally, I have profited enormously from Dr. Fisher's insight and analysis.

Last but not least, I also want to thank my editor at Sage, C. Deborah Laughton, for her patience, humor, and encouragement of this project.

INTRODUCTION

This book tells a simple story about a simple man, my grandfather. The story is based upon his diaries, which were started in July 1938 and completed in November 1950, shortly before his death.

To tell this story, I have divided the book into three parts. Part I provides the background. Included in Part I are the circumstances under which I obtained the diaries; the obstacles regarding translating the diaries; the information-gathering required for the names and locales; the context of immigration; and the theory (or biases) that guided this project.

Part II provides the diaries and interpretations. These diaries, I should note, are neither eloquent nor profound. Instead, they are fragmentary and austere. Thus, the interpretations (done in collaboration with Chana Held) are kept simple, in an effort to elucidate and inform, rather than analyze and extrapolate.

Part III of this book examines both the broader context of the diaries per se and the relevance of such material for the social sciences. This section will also explore the following two rationales for case study research: (a) Adjunct to Induction and (b) Extrapolations from Popper's Philosophy of Science.

PART I

The Background

On February 2, 1985, I received a package. It contained three handwritten books, plus a note from my mother: "I found these in a closet. They belonged to your father. They're your grandfather's (Samuel Abramson's) diaries. Written in Hebrew."

Interesting. I never knew that my grandfather kept a diary. And furthermore, I can't read Hebrew. So I put the diaries away in a drawer for several months, until I met Chana Held.

Chana was accepted into UCLA's Ph.D. program in psychology in March 1985. Subsequently, I learned that she was an Orthodox Jew and fluent in Hebrew. So I set up an appointment with her on July 24, 1985.

When Chana arrived, I showed her the diaries. She took one look and said, "This is not Hebrew. It's Yiddish. And I can't read Yiddish well enough to translate a whole diary."

Needless to say, I was disappointed. It was essential to have a competent Yiddish translator, someone with the ability and credentials to satisfy scientific requirements. And while meeting Chana was a fortuitous event—since she has gone on to make a major contribution to this project—I still needed a translator.

As an alternative, I decided to write a small grant, and hire a translator. I applied for intra-mural funding, in the form of a UCLA Academic Senate Grant, which was eventually approved.

Armed with funding, we made some new contacts, which led to two options: (a) a private translator, named Freida Beer; or (b) an agency, Language Service International. After obtaining estimates from Language Service International, we chose Freida. Her translation of 10 sample

pages was accurate (as attested by independent reviewers), easy to read, and psychologically sophisticated. Thus
we hired her in October 1985, and she completed her
translation in March 1986.

Once we could read the diary, it was apparent that some
background information was necessary. For example, a
brief description of Russia in the late nineteenth century
was essential. Furthermore, it was also obvious that we
needed to investigate whether information existed on a
tiny town called Kvarteri (where Samuel Abramson was
born), plus the larger towns of Sislovitch and Berestovich
(where Samuel Abramson spent much of his time).

On January 6, 1986, Chana met with Shimeon Brisman,
the Jewish bibliographer at UCLA's University Research
Library. Rabbi Brisman was very helpful and directed us
to a series of volumes known as the *Memorial Books*.
These books were compiled by Holocaust survivors for the
purpose of resurrecting memories of small towns and vil-
lages throughout Europe. (Lists of the *Memorial Books* can
be found in *Toledot Magazine*. Also, this list is updated by
Zachary Bakery, in his book, *From A Ruined Garden*.)

Since Samuel Abramson also mentioned the names of
several rabbis, we attempted to find records of these individuals as well. We examined the *Agudat HaRabbanim*, a
compilation of Orthodox Rabbis, and *The Annual Proceedings of the Rabbinic Assembly*, which covers Rabbis at the
Jewish Theological Seminary in New York. Similarly, to
complete our background research on Sislovitch, we also
consulted the Lippincott *Gazeteer*, which lists geographi-
cal locations, and Chester Cohen's book, *The Shtetl
Finder*. This latter book was particularly helpful because it
directed us to *Memorial Books* on Sislovitch and Bialystok.

Besides the information-gathering mentioned above, we
also investigated emigration records, plus Samuel Abramson's personal documents, such as photographs and his
marriage certificate.

Finally, we wanted a map of Russia, from the late nineteenth or early twentieth century, that included the town
Swislocz (Sislovitch). At the UCLA Map Library, we found
a Russian map, dating back to the 1880s. Although it was

written in Russian characters, the town names, such as Swislocz, were easy to identify.

As a result of this information-gathering we were also able to create (and include below) a simple description of both Sislovitch and the Jewish settlement residing therein. However, a cautionary remark is warranted. First, this section is neither a complete nor a rigorously scrutinized history (Bailyn, 1982; Barraclough, 1962; Dray, 1962; Higham, 1983; Kammen, 1980). Instead, it is sparse background material, derived from a small number of sources (Bein, 1941; Sachar, 1967; the *Memorial Books,* and the literature cited above) and designed merely to put the diaries in perspective and provide a very simple introduction.

SWISLOCZ

Samuel Abramson was born in 1885 in the town of Kvarteri, near the city of Swislocz, in Grodne Province.

Swislocz, which the Jews called Sislovitch, was established in the late fourteenth century by landowners named Pakosh. It transferred title in the seventeenth century to landowners named Krishpinow. And finally, in the eighteenth century, it became the property of the Tishkabitz nobility.

Sislovitch appealed to the Tishkabitz family, in particular Vitcenti Tishkabitz. It was Vitcenti who enlarged the town and designed an expansive marketplace, surrounded by houses. For a centerpiece, he installed a large bronze statue of a female warrior, brandishing a sword. This warrior, as myth would have it, was part of the town's defense. From her sword, lightning bolts would fly, creating fire and havoc for enemy intruders.

Sislovitch had five roads leading to and from the marketplace. The entrance of each road was framed in stone, which supported a large gate. Since the town itself was surrounded by either houses or ditches, Sislovitch had the option of closing its gates anytime it wanted, which it did every evening, stopping the flow either into or out of the city. Thus, Sislovitch existed as an independent and insulated little town near the Russian/Polish border.

Sislovitch had its share of commerce. On the east section of the marketplace, between Amstibuba and Rudevke streets, existed stores built of large stones. These stores were the focal point of the "merchant fairs" initiated several times a year by the Tishkabitz family. The announcement of a fair would go out, and the crowds would flow in, from both Russia and Poland. Presumably, everyone would profit, especially the merchants.

Vitcenti didn't limit himself to enhancing commerce. He built a public garden, complete with walking paths. And on the southwest part of the town, he also built a gymnasium, which was later converted into a seminary for teachers who sought work throughout the entire Grodne Province.

A synagogue was also eventually built in the northwest section of Sislovitch. And as the town swelled, low-cost housing soon appeared. Called *akapes* (the "pits"), these houses were built along the narrow side streets that bordered the ditches surrounding the town.

However, Sislovitch was not without its calamities. Fires destroyed large portions of the town on three separate occasions: in the 1830s; in the 1880s; and in the summer of 1910.

Jewish Settlement in Swislocz

Jews had been part of Sislovitch for several hundred years, as confirmed by legible tombstones. However, prior to the 1700s, the number of Jews in Sislovitch was very small. Their size increased when the town was transferred to the Tishkabitz family. Vitcenti's mercantile improvements provided the incentive. Thus, by 1847, the census listed 997 Jews in the township of Sislovitch, and by 1897, the census listed 2,086 Jews. This number is substantial when one considers that a large number of Jews were also emigrating to England, America, and Argentina.

As Sislovitch prospered, so did the Jews. At first, the Jews were primarily day laborers or small shopkeepers; however, as commerce expanded, especially with the mercantile fairs, the Jews gained success not only as shopkeepers, but also in larger businesses, such as hotels and taverns.

In the 1830s, the business atmosphere changed. A fire ravaged the shops, and the Tishkabitz family vanished, frightened off during the Polish Rebellion. Thus, the fairs ceased, and the economy slipped. To offset the changing economic climate, the Jews learned a new trade: leather-making. At first, their product was mediocre—durable but not attractive. With time, they improved, especially after they brought in experts from Germany to help them develop their craft.

Eventually, a number of prominent leather-makers emerged, such as Pinchas Brezenitzki, Sender Mintz, Eliyahu Rubin (and sons), and Itshe Pinchas Levintshick. And by the end of the nineteenth century, the tiny town of Sislovitch could boast 10 leather factories, employing several hundred workers. This circumstance, of course, altered the life-style of many Jews. The rich got richer, and so did the leather-workers. And to help spend that money, several enterprising Jews established the first "five and dime stores" (zdenovitch and ilinski villis). Now it was possible to buy shoelaces, water urns, salty fish, sardines, expensive hats, and prayerbooks—all in the same store.

And what of Samuel Abramson? What was his life like in Sislovitch, in late-nineteenth-century Russia?

Unfortunately, little is known. The details are missing from Samuel's diary, and there are no other family records. Thus, at best, all we can offer are some general notions about Jews in late-nineteenth-century Russia that may or may not have relevance to Samuel Abramson.

For example, Russian Jews were a fairly cohesive group. Their religion, customs, and community were combined into a highly organized society, which was essential to Jewish well-being. On the other hand, the Jews were also over-taxed, oppressed, and often vilified. Worse yet, they were subject to random killings, known as pogroms. Thus, although drawn to Russian sentiments, most Jews remained separate.

For these Jews, perhaps even for Samuel, there was consolation in religion. They believed that strict adherence to religious observation and ritual provided them with a sense of control and a feeling of security and contentment. Furthermore, the overt expression of their religion required them to assist other Jews by caring for the sick, feeding the poor, and sheltering the homeless, all of which created a strong feeling of community.

However, despite the lofty aspirations of religious commitment, Russian Jews were Russian subjects. Thus, as Russia prospered—and as Russia failed—so did the Jews. Consequently, Samuel Abramson's fate has as much relevance to his religion as to the politics of his country.

While Jewish welfare in Russia was marginal at best, life under Alexander II (1855-1881) was relatively benign. Of course, despite progress, discrimination still existed. Thus in 1861, when newly emancipated serfs needed land to cultivate, it was taken from the Jews. And when peasants needed a new village, this land was also taken from the Jews. Consequently, as more and more Jewish land was confiscated, the Jews were banished to city slums and *shtetls*.

On the positive side, Tzar Alexander II stopped the pogroms (enforced killings) and the excessive taxation, so the Jews were more likely to stay alive—and more likely to have extra money. For these two favors, the Jewish communities extended considerable gratitude and loyalty to Alexander II.

Unfortunately, however, all good things come to an end, and so did Alexander II. He was assassinated in 1881 and his death was followed by extreme violence and chaos. Many Russian peasants blamed the Jews for this tragic outcome and, as reparation, publicly victimized innocent Jews.

Although this violence was short-lived, two proclamations introduced in the following year would have enormous impact upon the Jews. One affected Jewish participation in the army. The other affected the number of Jews allowed to attend secondary school.

Alexander II had introduced a regulation that reduced Jewish military service to 4 years (it had been 25 years, starting at 12 or 13 years of age). Moreover, this regulation had not always been enforced, and there had been a variety of legal exemptions.

However, in 1886 (the year after Samuel was born), the Jewish draft was summarily reinstated. Since army life often entailed brutal beatings and forced conversion to Christianity, many Jews resisted, often escaping by emigrating. To counteract this, the Russian government established a policy whereby Jewish families would have to pay enormous fines when their sons failed to report for military service. This further impoverished an already impoverished minority.

Equally disturbing was the second regulation, a quota on the number of Jews allowed to attend secondary school. This deprived the Jews of not only education but also the exemption from military service that was often granted to secondary school graduates.

Consequently, Russian Jews wanted to escape, and emigration was the practical solution. Practical in the sense that it was expedient, but by no means routine. Most Jews were very poor; 40% of the population had no marketable skills. Similarly, although 2 million Jews emigrated from Russia in the first 33 years after Alexander II's assassination, the number of Jews left in Russia remained constant because the increased birth rate, and medical services provided by Jewish communities, kept the population replenished.

It was against this backdrop that Samuel Abramson left Russia, in 1903. He was 18 years old, a boy, in search of a dream to be found in America, the land of opportunity.

Perhaps Samuel concluded it was now time to get out. Russia was politically and economically unstable, and blatantly anti-Semitic. Also, his father's land had been confiscated (as indicated in family records); his educational possibilities were limited; and his military service was just around the corner. Thus, it appears that Samuel resolved to leave, presumably believing that life had to be better, especially in America.

THEORY AND BIASES

Before introducing the diaries, two additional issues need to be considered, both of which impact upon the manner in which these diaries are handled. The first is my theory concerning Russian Jewish immigration. This theory is particularly relevant to what I perceive the diary to confirm, as well as perhaps biasing what I highlight therein. Secondly, I want to also consider the personal biases, which undoubtedly influence how a grandson would reflect upon his grandfather's diaries. These biases, plus those of Chana Held, are certainly critical to the internal validity of this project and need to be exposed prior to our interpretations.

Theory

The factors that precipitated Samuel Abramson's emigration from Russia are not unique to Samuel, but are fairly typical of Russian Jewish immigrants. Emigration was usually the product of aversive or intolerable conditions, coupled with the expectation that better circumstances and opportunities existed elsewhere.

On the other hand, while emigration is an obvious and expedient solution for intolerable conditions at home, it does not necessarily obviate trauma and turmoil in the adopted homeland. Problems with a new language, the absence of marketable skills, discrimination, and family disintegration can also produce considerable hardships. Thus, it seemed reasonable to conceptualize emigration as a type of investment. I propose that Russian Jewish emigration can be conceptualized as an investment that has a tremendous short-run downside risk, but a potential for long-term sustained growth. That is, although Russian Jewish emigration was an expedient solution to problems at home, it yielded a plethora of obstacles in the adopted homeland, which in many ways offset the initial gains obtained by emigrating. However, as adaptation was achieved and future generations produced, substantial benefits of emigration were attained. According to this perspective, Russian Jewish emigration was a long-term investment, whose gains operated according to a U-shaped curve, whereby initial obstacles diminished rewards, but eventually, as a function of time, anticipated gains were produced. Thus, in many ways, the *merit* of the investment (i.e., emigration to America) was always viable, but the initial conditions were unstable, thereby delaying the eventual returns—in this case, greater religious, financial, and educational possibilities in the United States.

Simply stated, it is my belief that the true rewards of Russian Jewish emigration are not realized for several generations. Although the immigrant has clearly avoided the travails of early twentieth-century Russian tyranny, adapting to America without major resources is a considerable burden. This is especially true for a young person isolated from family. Thus, the degree of success or happiness achieved in the adopted homeland is usually diminished by several conditions, including the trials and tribulations of escaping from Russia, the resultant poverty, a language barrier, discrimination, the absence of marketable skills, and so forth. Furthermore, these conditions (and their psychological sequelae) are often not surmounted in the next generation because, quite simply, their impact was so pervasive on the Russian Jewish immigrant parents. Therefore, the long-term profit is usually realized several generations away. And in this regard, Russian Jewish emigration is perhaps best described as an act of courage, since the anticipated rewards were often symbolic and much delayed.

Interpreter Bias

It is often said that psychological interpretations tell you more about the interpreter than about the person being interpreted. In this particular project, these suspicions are certainly warranted because of the personal relationships involved. And while this issue is dealt with more substantively in Part III (in terms of internal validity), we felt that it might be helpful if both interpreters (Paul Abramson and Chana Held) provided statements on personal issues that could minimize our objectivity. Although we have striven to limit the intrusion of these issues when elaborating upon the diary, these statements should give the reader sufficient information for judging our success.

Paul Abramson

Although Samuel Abramson was my grandfather, I never knew him. He died when I was 11 months old. Also, strangely enough, no one ever talked about him. He was survived by three sisters, a wife, and two children. One child was my father, Leonard. The other child was my Aunt Sylvia. Paradoxically, despite these family members, my grandfather Samuel remained a mystery to me—an elderly man in a photograph—remote, unavailable, and historic.

The diary changed that. My grandfather Samuel came alive. He had thoughts, feelings, and experiences. And furthermore, he became part of my family, someone with a history, a sense of being, not merely an image in a photograph.

Unfortunately, as my grandfather became alive in his diary, my objectivity correspondingly diminished. Grandfather Samuel became a "real" member of my family, and as such, was treated differently.

How could this contaminate my interpretations? First of all, I might inflate the significance of this material. Second, I might show more interest in the material than it deserves. Thus, throughout the elaboration of the diary, I tried to keep both of those tendencies in check. Moreover, I have also asked two of my colleagues to review this material and document the extent of contamination.

Similarly, I am also aware that I am prone to pathologize Samuel. Though I never knew him, I knew his offspring (my father) well.

I did not like my father. He was frequently volatile, impulsive, and out-of-control. He also had a raging temper and was plagued with obsessional fears. Furthermore, I never felt that my father was a *nice* man. He seemed stuck in the role of "master sergeant," his rank in the army. Finally, he failed miserably in business, losing the two enterprises he started.

On the positive side, my father was very bright, was a gifted musician, and could occasionally be charming. Furthermore, he had creative entrepreneurial ideas that, unfortunately, never went anywhere.

Since my father did not "spring from the cosmos," I have assumed—whether fair or not—that there was a causal relationship between his behavior and that of my grandfather. Thus, as a consequence, I am predisposed to malign Samuel Abramson.

Is that fair? No, it is probably not. I would certainly resent any causal comparison between myself and my father; yet, I know that such comparisons are warranted. Leonard was my father, and I am part of him. However, since I am not the embodiment of Leonard's pathological side, it is equally possible that Leonard was not the embodiment of his father. Consequently, I have also tried to check my tendency to pathologize my grandfather. And once again, I have had colleagues review my interpretations to help me minimize the extent of this contamination.

Chana Held

I am observant of Orthodox Jewish Law (*halacha*), and find the *halachic* lifestyle very satisfying. Furthermore, the study of Torah, and its transmission from generation to generation, is exceedingly precious to me. As a consequence, my greatest challenge in objectivity was trying to understand what "being Jewish" meant to Samuel. At first, I was quite disappointed that Samuel was not a Shabbos observer. Thus, I have been concerned that I would minimize the profound meaning Judaism would have for Samuel, because he was not fully committed to *halacha*. Moreover, I had to remind myself that Samuel's life story was not necessarily a typical tale of assimilation. Even if Samuel did become less ritually observant, he may have remained emotionally and culturally committed to a very meaningful Judaism.

Also, I tried to remain open to the possibility of reverse assimilation. For instance, if Samuel came to America as a non-Sabbath observer, he was presumably fully prepared to work on Saturday to get ahead. However, the possibility existed that as Samuel's success grew (thereby providing more security), he would become a more ritually observant Jew.

However, as I became increasing involved in this project, another issue surfaced. I became concerned that I might glorify Samuel's incidental actions, so as to make him seem more devoted to Jewish values. Consequently, I have tried to he aware of all of these potential biases in an effort to maintain balance in my interpretations. Additionally, colleagues were also asked to review and comment upon the extent of this bias.

Another source of bias also existed. Since Paul Abramson is my graduate advisor—as well as a person that I like, admire, and respect—I was concerned that I would inflate his grandfather's uniqueness and brilliance. However, Paul and I were able to minimize this tendency by working independently while writing the first draft. I would write my ideas and commentary, and leave them in Paul's faculty mailbox. Thus, I became distanced from the intimacy of Samuel's being Paul's grandfather, and from a desire to flatter or impress Paul. Once again, this potential bias was also reviewed by colleagues.

Finally, as a psychology graduate student, I shared Paul's concern regarding the tendency to pathologize Samuel. In analyzing the diary, I of course wanted to understand Samuel's defenses and limitations. However, I also wanted to understand Samuel's psychological growth and personal transformations. Thus, it is my hope that Samuel has been analyzed with justice and compassion, as a multidimensional person. Again, reviewers have been asked to evaluate the extent of our achievement in this regard.

PART II

The Diaries
and Interpretations
(Written with Chana Held)

A HISTORY OF MY LIFE

By Samuel Abramson

I was born on the 21st day of Cheshvan, in 1885. It was in a courtyard in the town of Kwartery, near Sislovitch, Grodne Province, in Russia.

I received my education in the cheders of the nearby towns of Sislovitz and Berestovitch. This type of education was common for the children in our area. Furthermore, I lacked for nothing as a child, because my grandfather Lieb (may he rest in peace) treated me very lovingly . . . he was very good to me.

When I started learning Gemorah, I moved to Bialystok, where I "ate days," like all the other boys. My Aunt Hodel, who lived there, was very good to me. However, after living in Bialystok for a while, I returned to my home.

I already knew some Polish and German, but felt the urge to know Russian, so I enrolled in the gymnasium. I learned to read and write Russian very fluently. Then I went to work in a nearby factory. It was extremely difficult, and after a year or so, I decided it was not for me, and returned home. I opened a little business—trading with the local landowner—and making a few dollars. Soon however, I received a steamship ticket for America, from my loving cousin Yechiel.

And so I left Europe, passed through Antwerp, and boarded the ship Fatherland *for America. For 14 days I was seasick, suffering agonies. Finally, God helped, and I arrived in America—in the Golden Land.*

As the reader will note, we have sectioned this diary into short narratives. This strategy should enable us to make

interpretations or elaborations upon a manageable set of
data. Also, short narratives should make it easier for the
reader to remember, or recognize, words or passages that
we have chosen for interpretation.

Two types of interpretations are provided. In most cases,
the interpretation will involve elaboration upon Jewish
customs, Jewish phrases, Jewish history, or the Abramson family. Occasionally, however, speculative interpretations will also be offered. This speculation will be
presented cautiously, with the usual warnings relevant to
such inferences.

In 1885, the 21st day of *Cheshvan* would correspond to
the English date of October 30 or 31. *Cheshvan* is one of
the few Hebrew months in which there are no Jewish holidays. Moreover, throughout the diary, Samuel observes
his birthday according to the Hebrew calendar. As such,
the English date varies each year. However, when Samuel
states his age, it would appear that he was born in 1884,
and that his English birthday was November 11 or 12.

Why the confusion? Obviously, differences between the
English and Hebrew calendars contributed to the discrepancy. However, perhaps equally at play, is the fact that
Samuel is straddling two distinct cultures of Russian Jew
and recent American immigrant. Throughout Samuel's life,
he affirms his Judaism by celebrating his birthday according to the Hebrew calendar, suggesting that although he
lived in America, his internal "clock" was primarily Jewish.

What year was Samuel born? And why the discrepancy
in the date? As mentioned above, he states that he was
born in 1885, yet his age suggests otherwise. Obviously,
the most parsimonious answer is that the discrepancy
was a simple and unintentional mathematical error, re-
sulting from the confusion of immigration.

Kwatery is located approximately 60 kilometers directly
east of Bialystok, 10 kilometers north of Sislovitch, and 6
kilometers south of Berestovitch. Bialystok, by the way, is
now part of Poland.

"Born in a courtyard" (*arenda*) may have several meanings. On the one hand, it may signify the circumstances of
his birth. However, it may also imply that his family managed

an estate. *Arenda* were large parcels of land owned by absentee noblemen. This land was often farmed, but occasionally also contained a tavern that sold liquor to the local populace and provided lodging for travelers. Typically, the landlord would live in Paris or Warsaw, but would hire a Jewish man to oversee his estate (and supervise the non-Jewish indigent workers). In this circumstance, there would be one Jewish family per *arenda,* and not more than one or two other Jewish families in Kwatery.

Samuel also states that he "lacked for nothing as a child." We find this surprising and rather hard to believe, given the status of Jews in late-nineteenth-century Russia. We note that he doesn't mention his mother and father. What were his parents like? Were they loving, devoted, and caring? And if so, why does he mention only the love from his grandfather Lieb?

While a grandparent's love can certainly increase the quality of a child's life, it obviously does not compensate for parental affection. Thus, we wonder whether the failure to mention the love from his parents was not unintentional.

"May he rest in peace" is an expression that Samuel uses throughout the diary. It reflects the value that Jewish tradition places upon showing respect for the deceased. "May he rest in peace" is used for "ordinary" Jews, in contrast to the expression "may his name be for a blessing," which is used for very pious or learned individuals. Finally, such expressions are part of Jewish customs and do not reflect a special piety by the user.

Within the Jewish culture, education is a highly valued asset. Thus in Russia, when Jewish families were isolated, they provided education by either hiring a tutor or sending their children elsewhere. Samuel Abramson's family chose the latter. He was sent to Sislovitch and Berestowitch, each of which had approximately 2,000 Jewish residents.

When Samuel started learning *Gemorah* (at approximately 8 to 10 years of age), he indicates that he moved to Bialystok. *Gemorah* is the Yiddish word for *Talmud.* The *Talmud* contains commentary and discussion on the *Mishnah* (Jewish legal texts) by Jewish scholars from the third to fifth centuries. Bialystok, incidentally, was a major Jewish center in Eastern Europe. In 1897 almost 27,000 Jews lived there, constituting 64% of the population.

Since Jewish families who sent their children away for study were often unable to afford room and board, such children usually had to "eat days," which means eating meals at a different home every day of the week. While Samuel undoubtedly slept at his Aunt Hodel's house, she presumably could not afford to feed him. Consequently, "eating days" was a community-supported custom that was an indirect contribution to the local *yeshivas* (places of study).

Since Samuel lived in Russia, it might seem odd that he could not speak Russian. However, this circumstance is not surprising. Prior to 1815 Grodne Province was part of the Kingdom of Poland; consequently, the primary language was still Polish. Also, since German was the language of the intelligentsia, many Russian Jews liked to think that they knew German. Russian Jews could often speak Yiddish, and as such, could understand some German; however, most of them had very little (if any) contact with the German language, culture, or citizens.

When Samuel "enrolled in the gymnasium," he was presumably 15 years of age. Although equivalent to high school, the gymnasium provided a rigorous secular education, with competitive academic standards. Although some Jews chose to attend the gymnasium, most Jews refused. Since the gymnasium provided an alternative to traditional Orthodox *yeshivas,* it was perceived as encouraging assimilation. Not surprisingly, many Jews resented this perspective.

Given Samuel's strong Jewish identity, why did he choose to go to a Gymnasium? Certainly there must have been resistance, if not within his family, then within the Jewish community. As such, perhaps this circumstance suggests that Samuel was capable of going against the grain. Presumably, he perceived education as a nondenominational asset, that is, a virtuous and noble endeavor, regardless of orientation. For example, if Samuel could enhance his mind, he would ultimately become a better person, and perhaps (he rationalized) a better Jew. This perspective, by the way, is consistent with the "German Enlightenment movement."

It is interesting to note that when Samuel deviated from an Orthodox religious perspective, he initiated an inevitable chain of events, that is, the Abramson family ultimately lost a strong religious tradition. For instance, when Samuel arrived in the United States, he joined the Conservative Judaism movement, rather than the Orthodox movement. Not surprisingly, his son (Leonard) went one step farther and became involved in Reform Judaism. Finally, two generations later, his grandson (Paul) has furthered that gesture by remaining agnostic.

Samuel also indicates that he worked in a factory. Presumably, this was a leather factory in Sislovitch, where the working conditions were atrocious, including 16-hour workdays in dim, impoverished facilities. However, Samuel goes home and "opens a little business—trading with the local landowner." Perhaps Samuel had rented some agricultural land on the *arenda,* and organized a labor force of non-Jewish workers to harvest it. In any event, shortly thereafter, he received a steamship ticket to America.

At the turn of the century, steamship tickets to America had to be purchased with American currency. Once purchased, they were sent to Russia through an agency in Germany. Families who could afford such tickets were usually relatively well established in the United States. Thus, Samuel was by no means the first member of his family to sever Jewish European traditions. In fact, many Jews left Russia following the pogroms of 1881, which had the adverse effect of severely taxing the Jewish European organizations designed to assist emigrants. Consequently, many naive emigrants were tricked and harassed. Furthermore, most emigrants had to sneak across the Russian border to avoid anti-Semitic peasants, the Russian military, and Russian government officials. Once across the border, Jewish emigrants would travel to Hamburg, Berlin, or Antwerp to seek advice from Jewish agencies. However, by the time Samuel emigrated in 1903, the procedures were more routine. Emigrants usually took a train across the border, knew exactly where to stay, and already had possession of their tickets. In 1903 the steamship ticket from Antwerp to New York cost $34.

As Samuel indicates, he experienced terrible seasickness on his trip. This was not uncommon. Some emigrants would spend the whole trip consumed by intense and continual vomiting. Adding to this misery were cramped sleeping quarters, inedible food, and inadequate toilet facilities. Thus, many emigrants arrived at Ellis Island in a weak and dehydrated condition.

*   *   *

It was 1903 when I came to America, to Uncle Judah and Aunt Ada. They lived in an apartment on the 4th floor on Eldridge Street, on the Lower East Side. My dear cousin Yechiel immediately took me to a clothing store, and outfitted me with a new suit of clothes and hat. Thus, I became an Americanetz, and I felt very good.

Then we began the search for a job. I wound up learning the cap-maker trade in Elizabeth Street. However, sitting constantly at a sewing machine was horrible. I was not used to this, so I left for Norwalk, Connecticut, to seek my luck there.

I lived in Norwalk with my Aunt Chana. And to make money, I became a peddler, selling from door to door. But this job was not successful. I could barely speak English and hardly knew my way around Norwalk. And worse yet, I couldn't find anything else, because I was a greener. However, thank God, I didn't peddle for long, as I was offered work at the Norwalk Lock Shop.

Unfortunately, I also had a miserable time at this job, even though I worked at the lock shop for a couple of years. The other people made fun of my English. Thus, I realized that if I wanted to improve my situation, I had to learn English. So, I enrolled in night school, and was able to learn the language fairly rapidly, which made me very happy.

I (Paul Abramson) barely remember Yechiel and have no recollection of an Uncle Judah and Aunt Ada. When I met

Yechiel, he was a very old man. I was 8, and my family journeyed to Brooklyn to visit relatives. It was a hot and oppressive summer day. As I remember, we had to climb two flights of stairs, through a dark and musty hallway. At the top was a gentle, shrunken man who spoke softly in a foreign language. This was Yale (i.e., Yechiel), a cousin and good friend of my grandfather's.

I now regret that I did not make more of this trip. Yale was one of the many peripheral relatives who paraded through my childhood. Invariably, I could not figure out who these people were, and was usually annoyed by their intrusion. However, as I read this diary, I was excited by the intimate connection between Yale and my grandfather.

Samuel indicates that his first task in America was to get "outfitted with a new suit of clothes and hat." Why? Were his old clothes worn out? Or did he dress like a Russian? If the new clothes made him *Americanetz*, it suggests that his old clothes were distinctively Russian.

What does Samuel mean that he "became an *Americanetz*" as a consequence of changing clothes? Is he stating that "clothes make the man"? Is this a superficial assumption that changes in the exterior "shell" produce changes in the internal person? Or perhaps, Samuel was excited. Maybe he felt that with new clothes, at least he looked American at first glance.

Once again, working in a factory had little appeal to Samuel. Therefore, he set out for Norwalk, Connecticut. This suggests two circumstances. First, Samuel was unwilling to settle for just anything. He believed that America was the golden land, and obviously, nobody got rich working in a sewing factory. So Samuel left. He was young and perhaps he believed that he had many other options.

Second, having other options suggests that Samuel had sufficient family in the United States. He could pack up and leave New York, and stay with a relative in Norwalk, Connecticut. Norwalk, Connecticut, by the way, became his home and the birthplace of his son (Leonard) and grandson (Paul).

"To seek my luck" is an interesting phrase. The process of emigration, as mentioned earlier, is ultimately a risky investment, much like gambling. Perhaps, according to Samuel, you roll the dice and keep your fingers crossed.

It was fascinating to me (Paul Abramson) to learn that my grandfather was a peddler, especially to imagine him as a young man, with a funny-looking cart (i.e., pots clanging, brooms and brushes sticking out at weird angles, and so on). And going door-to-door—without knowing English—certainly took guts (or was simply foolish). However, as Samuel notes, he was a *greener*, and opportunities were scarce. Incidentally, *greener* was the Yiddish word for "greenhorn," a common reference to recent immigrants. Moreover, *oysgrinen zikh*, to cease being a greenhorn, was a favorite Yiddish slogan.

Eventually, "thank God," Samuel was offered a job at the Norwalk Lock Shop. Homage to God is common throughout this diary. Samuel thanked God for every favor and believed that God would ultimately alleviate his suffering. Is this perspective the consequence of his religion, his Russian Jewish heritage, or his person? Probably all three. Although Samuel took considerable initiative in his actions, his perspective on life and the world was strongly grounded in the Jewish religion. Also, given the dismal *shtetls* of Russia, most Russian Jews sought spiritual salvation, rather than personal or political intervention. As a consequence, though Samuel was embarking on a personal quest in the United States, God was an intimate companion.

Unfortunately, the lock shop was miserable. Moreover, people made fun of Samuel because he couldn't speak English. Consequently, he devised a plan. He would learn English, which would both improve his job prospects, and keep him from being ridiculed. Thus, once again, Samuel perceived secular education as the vehicle of progress.

*   *   *

Now I started to think, "How I could help my family back home in Russia?" Fortunately, I was able to send a steamship ticket for my sister Rachel. I'll never forget her arrival. It was winter and terribly cold that year. However, I was delighted beyond description to see her, my beloved sister.

She brought loving regards from all, and we spent hours talking about the family.

After Rachel arrived, it gave me indescribable satisfaction to come home from work and find her awaiting me. Also, it was wonderful to have someone to confide in.

With newfound courage, we both worked hard and saved a few pennies. Eventually, we were able to send steamship tickets (for America) to our parents and two younger sisters.

Yidl, our brother, had bad eyes. Consequently, he remained home in Russia, with our old grandmother. He died when the Russian Revolution broke out. My heart hurts whenever I think of him. He believed that the Russian Revolution would bring a new era of human freedom, and was willing to die for it.

Patiently, my sister and I awaited the arrival of our family. And when they finally arrived, a new life began for us. We, my sister and I, suffered a great deal, because we didn't have our own home. For example, Rachel lived with Tante Gittle, but had to clean her whole house, after finishing a hard day's work at her job. Also, I didn't get along with Tante Chana, and lived elsewhere.

However, we were the luckiest people in the world when our loving mother arrived and started to run the household. Everything was so sweet and dear. Our younger sisters went to school, and I changed jobs.

At first, I worked in Sam Roodner's shop, then I left and went to work at Schacter's Grocery, and then at Louis Djesseloffs. At that time, we were living at 15 Orchard Street in South Norwalk. And as the family gradually adjusted, we all became very happy.

Although he fled Russia, Samuel was strongly connected to his family. Isolation in America probably strengthened this tie. Thus, Samuel was determined to "help his family back home." As it turned out, "help" meant "escape." Instead of sending money home, he brought his family to America, which, by the way, was a considerable feat. Samuel was a peddler/lock shop employee who saved enough money to bring his sister to America. Shortly thereafter, he and his sister (who presumably had a menial job) saved enough money to bring their parents and two siblings over. Additionally, they arranged for accommodations for a family of six.

Why did Samuel choose Rachel first? Perhaps they were closest when growing up. Her arrival in the United States was certainly an unforgettable event. Samuel's diary was started 20 years after he emigrated, yet Rachel's arrival is still crystal clear in his memory. Additionally, it appears that Rachel had the desire and capacity to work, which facilitated immigration for the entire family.

The impact of Rachel's arrival suggests that Samuel was depressed and isolated. Rachel became his confidant and provided him with "newfound courage." Why did he need additional courage? Was he despairing? Thinking about going back? Giving up? Or were his relatives less than supportive? If so, he may have needed a confidant. Also, perhaps his expectations for success and happiness were inflated, and the golden land was less than ideal. Did he make a mistake? Was it his fault?

Fortunately, however, Rachel helped. Together, they saved their "pennies," and were able to bring their family to America. But did they literally save pennies? Tickets, and immigration, certainly cost more than pennies, so why reduce the amount to the lowest denominator? Perhaps, since saving the money was a slow and depressing prospect, Samuel wanted to convey the magnitude of their task. Obviously, in order to afford the tickets, Samuel must have made enormous sacrifices, which necessarily affected his adjustment and satisfaction. Moreover, although it was a noble gesture, such sacrifices can also be emotionally devastating, which in turn might produce some hidden anger and resentment.

Why did Yidl (i.e., Edel) stay behind? Was it "bad eyes"? Or perhaps his commitment to the Russian Revolution? We believe the latter. Abramson family legend credits Yidl with the authorship of a book on revolutionary ideals. Moreover, since he died in the Russian Revolution, it suggests that Yidl stayed for political, rather than medical reasons. Why does Samuel imply otherwise? Perhaps, it was survivor guilt. Samuel may have blamed himself and felt that he should have been more persuasive in convincing Yidl to leave Russia. On the other hand, it is also likely that Samuel and Yidl didn't get along. Maybe they differed politically and grew apart. In this case, Samuel would be less invested in Yidl's emigration. However, when Yidl died in Russia, perhaps Samuel blamed himself.

Samuel states that he "patiently" awaited the arrival of his family. We find this hard to believe. People who are isolated and depressed are usually "anxiously" awaiting loved ones. Furthermore, since Samuel and Rachel were having difficulty with relatives, it would seem that patience would be impossible. Thus, it appears that Samuel tends to minimize obvious areas of stress.

Once the rest of the family immigrated to the United States, everything was "sweet and dear." Moreover, Samuel was the luckiest person on earth because his "loving mother" arrived. But what about his father (who also arrived)? Did Samuel's father not bring luck? Or was his father not loving? It is interesting to note that his father is the only member of his immediate family not mentioned. We wonder why.

*   *   *

Around this time, a grocery store became available on Bouton Street in South Norwalk, for $500 cash. We had saved some money, and after conferring with that great and good person (and everyone's friend) Philip Slominsky (may he rest in peace), we purchased this store. Slominsky gave us a loan for $200 toward the purchase, and I was now in business.

Business was good, and the neighborhood grew, as there was much immigration. Also, I learned to speak Hungarian because it went well with our business.

Our family moved to Bouton Street and lived together very happily. And as business became better and better, we bought a house at 9 Bouton Street, paid $500, and moved in.

Unfortunately, another grocery store opened on Ely Avenue, and our business began going down. It took a year's time, and eventually, nothing was left of our business. I just couldn't compete, and things became very bad for us. At that time, I was already married, and had a lovely wife and a 1-year-old daughter.

Because of the downfall of my business, I became ill with disappointment. Nothing else was in the offing. I couldn't make a living or obtain credit. The grocery store went almost completely under, and I was in deep trouble.

I had to struggle along, and there was no one to help. I was so ill, I couldn't work. My beautiful wife suffered much, seeing me so ill. I went to many doctors, and no one seemed to understand why I had these attacks and spells.

One day however, a good friend, Leib Pincus, recommended Dr. Emmanuel Brodski of Westport, Connecticut. And thank God, after going to him, I began to feel better, even though it took a long time before I fully recovered.

Samuel was depressed ("ill with disappointment"). He felt despair ("I was in deep trouble"), inertia ("so ill, I couldn't work") and helplessness ("no one seemed to understand why I had these attacks and spells"). Moreover, the depression persisted ("it took a long time before I fully recovered"), until Dr. Brodski intervened.

Who was Dr. Brodski? A newspaper clipping in Samuel's scrapbook indicates that Dr. Brodski was a psychiatrist. Born in Russia on December 22, 1878, Emmanuel Brodski received his medical training at the University of Zurich. Shortly thereafter, he was the assistant superintendent of Saint Urban's sanitorium in Switzerland. Eventually, Dr. Brodski emigrated to the United States, residing in Connecticut. In 1913 he established a private practice in Westport, Connecticut, and acted as assistant superintendent of the Westport sanitorium. In 1917 Dr. Brodski moved to Bridgeport, Connecticut.

Why was Samuel depressed? Obviously, the failure of his business was the precipitating factor. He borrowed money, took a risk, and came up empty. Moreover, Samuel was encumbered with a home and family, thereby accentuating his obligations. Not surprisingly, he was despondent. Yet, the depression appears chronic and debilitating, and presumably something more than an acute or transient crisis. Perhaps, Samuel's depression was being fueled by other dynamics.

Samuel was paying a heavy price for failure. He felt lost and inert. His wife suffered, and "there was no one to help." Moreover, Samuel was the victim of "attacks and spells" that seemed refractory to medical treatment. Did Samuel deserve this punishment? Perhaps, at an unconscious level, he felt that he did. This was his just rewards. Samuel left Russia, for the golden land, and eventually brought the rest of his family with him. But what happened? Was Samuel success-ful? No, the business failed. Worse yet, when Samuel in-flated his prospects, he had the entire family expecting immediate success. Unfortunately, fate proved otherwise. Perhaps, in Samuel's case, he attached his self-identity to his business acumen. Accordingly, the failure of his busi-ness meant the failure of Samuel, and the collapse of the Abramson dreams, which is certainly a depressing thought.

Why did Samuel carry this burden? Was it his choice, or was he pressured into responsibility? We believe the lat-ter. Samuel was the oldest son, the standard-bearer, the child expected to succeed. And furthermore, when Samuel came to America, he was the trailblazer, in search of free-dom and prosperity. But what about Samuel's feelings? Was he loved and supported? Was he nurtured and appre-ciated as a child? His diary might be suggesting otherwise. For example, it appears that he was the vehicle for pros-perity. His personal identity, and his family's expecta-tions, were attached to his affluence. Unfortunately, if true, this precipitates a vicious cycle. If one fails in busi-ness, one fails in life. Furthermore, if one succeeds in business, happiness is by no means insured. Freud's the-ory is perhaps instructive in this regard. Freud believed that happiness is the fulfillment of a childhood wish. And children don't instinctively wish for money. Instead, they wish for love, nurturance, companionship, and so on.

Did Samuel wish for love? This is never made explicit, but the diaries might be suggesting otherwise. For in-stance, Samuel's feelings about his courtship, his mar-riage, and the birth of his daughter are absent from his narrative. Was this intentional? Was Samuel making a point? Perhaps he felt that he gave the engagement, the marriage, and the birth of his daughter their due accord. On the other hand, maybe some of these milestones, such as his marriage, were relatively uneventful.

However, Samuel's scrapbook presents a different picture. His marriage, for instance, received considerable coverage in the local newspapers. The headline read: "Springwood Merchant Marries Brooklyn Girl: Norwalk Largely Represented at Wedding of Samuel Abramson and Miss Esther Greenspan." This 71-line article described the bride (21-year-old Esther Greenspan, a seamstress from Brooklyn, New York) and groom (24-year-old Samuel Abramson); the ceremony (at Lincoln Palace Hall, Brooklyn, New York. "The building was elaborately decorated with flowers, plants, flags, etc., presenting a fine sight."); the clothing ("The bride looked very beautiful in a costume of White Duchess satin with an overdress of Irish point lace."); the guests ("guests were present from Boston, Philadelphia and other places, and telegrams of congratulations came from many friends"); and so on. Certainly, it was an elaborate occasion, which makes it an even more striking omission from Samuel Abramson's "life history."

How did a 24-year-old Russian immigrant, in the United States for only 6 years, receive such extraordinary newspaper coverage, which presumably necessitated sending a reporter from Norwalk, Connecticut, to a Brooklyn wedding? The following sentences, taken from the aforementioned article, provide a clue: "He is usually the first to answer an alarm of fire or give aid to the authorities in the search for lawbreakers. Among the many magnificent presents received by the couple was a set of silver knives and forks from the South Norwalk police force." Thus, it appears that Samuel was notable in his community as both a volunteer firefighter and a volunteer police officer. Moreover, recognition of his efforts were acknowledged in the form of a gift from his local police department.

What kind of person is a volunteer firefighter and a volunteer police officer? In Samuel's case, he appears to be altruistic and civic-minded. Additionally, Samuel may have also had a strong need to participate in heroic works, as a means of gaining acceptance and approval (perhaps from his father). Photographs of Samuel also suggest that he was physically tough—broad shoulders and squat body, with powerful forearms (see p. 165). Also, his cap is pulled down low, with a no-nonsense look, that is, the kind of guy who has the temperament for firefighting and law enforcement. Yet, Samuel did not chose either of these occupations for a career. Instead, he was a volunteer, aiding his community and establishing his reputation within this growing town.

I (Paul Abramson) had two reactions to this section. At first, it was hard for me to imagine that my grandfather was depressed. In my fantasy, my forbears were simple and uncomplicated, that is, stoic in adversity and appreciative of small pleasures. Obviously, my fantasy is naive and one-dimensional.

On the other hand, I was also "glad" that he was depressed. It was confirmation that something was wrong. And by implication, not only with my grandfather, but with my father as well. Quite frankly, I felt vindicated and relieved.

In addition, as a psychologist, it fascinated me that my grandfather went to a psychiatrist. It must have been a novel experience, especially in 1915. And what was Dr. Brodski's therapeutic orientation? What were the treatment sessions like? Was my grandfather hypnotized? Was medication used? Or did he undergo analysis? (Since Dr. Brodski trained in Zurich, I also enjoyed imagining that he was a colleague [or disciple] of Carl Jung.)

Finally, I was saddened by my grandfather's focus on business, to the exclusion of his immediate family. At least from this part of the diary, he seems to have had a narrow and self-limiting existence.

* * *

"My father took sick and died in 1917. In the meantime, a Mr. Novak moved to Bouton Street and opened a chicken market. Eventually, he approached me and offered to sell his chicken business for $300. I borrowed the necessary cash from my cousin Leventhal of Stamford, Connecticut. Thus, I bought the business, and a car, for a good price.

I then sold my grocery store and became a full-time chicken dealer. The times were good, and so was the business. Now, I finally felt revived.

My mother and two younger sisters moved to Stamford, Connecticut. It was there that my sister Rachel met her husband Sol. After they were married, they made a good living operating a clothing store and managing real estate. Also, my sister Jennie married Mr. Slavitt, and my sister Esther married Dr. Wollin. Finally, after all of these weddings, my mother moved back to South Norwalk.

The chicken business did very well. I exchanged my Ford for a Larabee truck, and was then able to go to the Norwalk market for chickens. Also, I was able to buy auto insurance for $5,000, plus another $5,000 for disability insurance.

My wife and I had to work very, very hard together at this business. However, we were satisfied. We were doing well, and could give our children special things, like music lessons: my daughter, piano; and my son, violin.

One day, I returned home as usual, but I found that my wife was taken to the hospital. While climbing a ladder, she had fallen and broken her leg. She had to remain "laid up" for 6 months and suffered great pain. I was heartbroken at her suffering. The children sat day and night with her at the hospital, keeping her company. When she finally came home, we were overjoyed. Our proverbs say: "A person is stronger than iron, and sometimes weaker than a fly."

The children were growing up very nicely. Sylvia, our daughter, finished high school. And Leonard, our son, is a good student. Business wasn't bad.

However, in 1928, I made the greatest mistake of my life. I bought a house on Flaxhill Road. This purchase brought me to rack and ruin. My wife begged me not to buy this house, but I didn't listen. And as luck would have it, business slowed down considerably. Thus, we lost the house, and had to move back to Bouton Street.

Afterwards, my wife found it too difficult to work at home, and at the store. She had to slow down. And because of my mistake, we all had a very bad time.

And to make matters worse, the business continued losing money. Thus, the crisis came. Nobody was earning any-

thing. My daughter, who was going to college, could hardly pay her tuition. This pained me terribly. Also, I couldn't pay my insurance, and had to cancel it.

No one was able, or wanted, to help me. Only God can help. It's a false world. However, that's life. A good, clever, and beautiful world isn't for all. But as long as we live, we must hope. And God will help "when the water seems to overwhelm us."

"My father took sick and died in 1917" is Samuel's sole reference to his father. A mere footnote of a nameless person, defined only by relationship, devoid of life, feeling, and elaboration.

Why the omission? Perhaps they didn't get along, and Samuel felt that "discretion was the better part of valor." On the other hand, at least from photographs, one could suggest that the family was matriarchal, with the power and control being vested in Samuel's mother. In these photographs, the father (Robert Abramson) seems passive and distant, perhaps only remotely connected with his children. Yet, Samuel's scrapbook again suggests otherwise. Robert Abramson (who died at 58) worked in his son's grocery store and the Obituary Record describes him as "well known" in Norwalk.

Although his grocery store failed, Samuel was capable of securing money to purchase a second business. And as the chicken business prospered, so did Samuel's psychological health. During the same period, it also appears that the Abramson daughters were married. It is interesting to note that the marriages were "profitable," that is, Rachel married a successful business person; Jennie married an attorney; and Esther married a physician. Perhaps the "prosperity" of the marriages warranted inclusion in the diary. On the other hand, since Samuel married a seamstress (who never learned to read English), it did not require mention in the "business of life."

Also omitted from the diary is the birth of Samuel's son, Leonard. Although Leonard was born in 1916, there is no record of his birth, infancy, or early childhood. Instead, he is first mentioned when he is old enough to be the recipient of violin lessons. Moreover, the reference to violin lessons is a mere footnote to Samuel's renewed profits. For instance, when Samuel's business was successful, he was capable of providing "special things, like music lessons" to his children.

While all parents want to provide "special things" for their children, Samuel's rationale seems self-defeating. Obviously, "giving" to children is not limited to material resources or periods of affluence. However, Samuel's relationship with his children, at least from this diary, appears measured in overt symbols of success and achievement. And while most parents are proud of the material resources they are capable of providing for their children, Samuel's narrative raises concern because it is void of the complementary function of satisfying the emotional or intimate needs of his kids. For instance, during an 18-year period, his daughter Sylvia is rarely mentioned ("one-year-old daughter"; "my daughter, piano"; "Sylvia, our daughter, finished high school"). Moreover, all three instances are void of emotional description.

However, where his wife Esther is concerned, Samuel eventually displays a strong emotional connection. Again, it is specific to adversity. Esther had broken her leg, and Samuel was "heartbroken at her suffering," and "overjoyed" when she came home. As a consequence, Samuel pondered the illusion of "strength."

Finally, Samuel "made the greatest mistake of (his) life." In 1928, when he was 43 years old, he bought a house that was beyond his means. "This purchase brought me to rack and ruin."

In the realm of "tragic mistakes," the inability to make payments on a house is an overstated offense. Certainly the loss of a cherished home is a depressing thought, but as the diary will attest, Samuel eventually prospered and bought another "cherished" house. Thus, why the hysteria? Was the Flaxhill Road house an impulsive purchase, ill-advised from the start and contrary to family advice? Was Samuel "punishing" himself for a foolish choice? Did his wife blame him for the failure and humiliation?

The most surprising aspect of this narrative is Samuel's failure to mention either the stock market crash or the

Great Depression. Samuel bought the Flaxhill Road home in 1928. Shortly thereafter, America was crippled by an economic crisis that undermined banks, business, and economic opportunities. Thus, it appears that Samuel was adversely affected by this decline. Yet, according to his narrative, his "greatest mistake" was personal and idiosyncratic (perhaps suggesting a narcissistic deficit?). Furthermore, Samuel's plaintive admonishment ("No one was able, or wanted to help . . . it's a false world . . . ") admits no recognition of the Great Depression. Instead, if you ignore the economic status of America, it appears that Samuel made a mistake, and to his chagrin, nobody was willing to help. Woe is Samuel.

Despite the economic adversity, Sylvia continued to attend college (Stone College, New Haven, Connecticut). It is interesting to note that Sylvia was paying her own tuition. And while the "crisis" made it such that she "could hardly pay," Sylvia persevered, and graduated in 1932 (having also been an Honor Student in the Sigma Mu chapter of Alpha Iota sorority). Thus, when evaluating Samuel's narrative, it is important to note that during the Depression, Samuel's business remained afloat and his daughter attended college.

*   *   *

My beloved daughter Sylvia has finished college. Thank God, I lived to see this. She had worked with my brother-in-law (Abe Slavitt), who is a lawyer, and then got a job teaching in a high school.

Times got a bit better, and my son started college. But I couldn't afford to pay, so he had drop out after a short time. This pained me deeply. I felt that I ruined my son's future.

Money makes the world go around. I alone am guilty for creating this situation. When times were good, I thought I'd always have money. And when times were bad, I didn't have a friend in the world. But God will help, and it'll be good again. Hopefully, it won't come too late.

The chicken business finally went bad. There was a chicken epidemic in Norwalk, Connecticut.

Afterwards, I tried to start another chicken business on Vodne Street, but, in the end, had to close it too. All the Italian immigrants went into the chicken business, and the competition ruined mine—down to the last penny.

In 1933, Prohibition was repealed. So I opened a saloon on Bouton Street. In the beginning, business wasn't bad. In fact, I made a living at it for a few years. However, over time, many other saloons opened, and I had to give it up.

This was also a pretty bad time. I couldn't find any other work. Eventually, however, I found a job at the cemetery. It wasn't what I wanted, but at least I earned a few dollars. Additionally, I was elected sexton of my lodge, which also paid me a few dollars.

At last, I got a job delivering meat for a butcher. Unfortunately, it was very hard to get accustomed to working for someone else, especially after being my own boss. But need breaks iron. I worked at this job for over a year. And however much I disliked the work, I was grateful to God that I was able to provide a few dollars for my family's support.

There is a blessing of thanksgiving, called *sheheyanu*, that Jews say when they arrive at a special occasion. The *sheheyanu* is translated as "Blessed art Thou, O Lord our God, King of the Universe, Who has kept us in life and has preserved us and enabled us to reach this time." This blessing is invoked for all major holidays, as well as the purchase (and wearing) of new clothes. The intent of *sheheyanu* is to thank God for being able to experience special moments. Thus, when Samuel writes, "Thank God I lived to see this" (in reference to Sylvia's graduation), he presumably had *sheheyanu* in mind. As indicated earlier, Jews put a premium on higher education, and college graduation would be a special moment.

Samuel indicates that Leonard started college. "But I couldn't afford to pay, so he had to drop out after a short time. This pained me deeply. I felt that I ruined my son's future."

This is a lie. Leonard flunked out of college at the end of his freshman year. His New York University transcripts attest to his grades (Fs) and terminated status. However

Samuel, and Leonard, maintained this hoax throughout their lifetimes. While relatives knew the true story (Samuel's sister, Esther Wollin, conceded that this was a "family secret"), Leonard's children learned the truth as a result of attempting to accumulate his personal records subsequent to his death in 1975.

Why the lie? And worse yet, why did Samuel take full responsibility? Was it self-punitive? Did Samuel have problems with separation and boundaries, such that he could not distinguish between his personal obligations and his son's responsibilities? If so, perhaps this is evidence of borderline or severe narcissistic thinking.

On the other hand, while it is probably true that Samuel had difficulty paying Leonard's tuition, why is Samuel's guilt so excessive and misplaced? Perhaps Samuel was convinced that his economic adversity undermined Leonard's desire and ability to study. (Of course, when faced with a similar situation, Sylvia paid her own way.) In either case, why did Samuel lie?

Perhaps the diary served as Samuel's atonement for "sins," that is, "Yes, Leonard flunked out of college, but certainly I'm also to blame. Therefore, since I'm partly at fault, I'll accept all responsibility. Finally, since I now blame myself, why blemish Leonard's record with the truth? Let's just say that he dropped out for financial reasons." Unfortunately, this convoluted logic—if true—is not fair to Samuel, or Leonard. Perhaps Samuel was so self-punitive and emotionally intertwined with his family that he failed to appreciate the culpability of others. In one instance, Samuel ignores the Great Depression. In the second instance, Samuel ignores the fact that his son flunked out of college (and also omits the positive fact that his son was an accomplished violinist, in a small orchestra called the "Paramount Collegians"). Could it be that Samuel often failed to appreciate his lack of control, or responsibility, over the actions of others? Certainly, Samuel fails to credit himself, or his family, with independence and freedom of action. Instead, it often seems as if Samuel perceives himself as the tragic centerpiece in a series of tumultuous family crises.

Eventually, the chicken business was discarded, and Samuel opened up a saloon. Called Sam's Tavern, the saloon offered weekly "Hungarian gypsy roasts," including a 12-piece Hungarian ensemble that played folk songs and *csardas*. Although a newspaper clipping in Samuel's scrapbook suggests that the tavern was successful, Samuel indicates that the tavern eventually failed. At which point, Samuel worked in a cemetery as a groundskeeper.

Samuel also mentions that he was elected "sexton" of his lodge. In the diary, Samuel uses the English word "sexton," instead of the traditional Yiddish word *shamash*. This suggests that his lodge was an Americanized synagogue group.

Generally, sexton was a salaried position within a synagogue. Responsibilities could include being secretary, messenger, carpenter, and fund-raiser. And during religious services, the sexton often determined the *aliyahs*, men who were called upon to offer blessings before and after reading the Torah. For instance, prior to reading a portion of the Torah, a member of the community is called up to the *bimah* (the table/stand where the Torah has been placed), and is asked to recite a blessing. Another blessing is recited after the portion has been read, and a new member is called upon to repeat the process. Thus, it is the job of the sexton to choose these men, and call them forward by their Hebrew name, that is, the son of their father's Hebrew name. For example, if Samuel's father's name was Yaacov, Samuel would be called up as "Shmuel ben (son of) Yaacov." It is also interesting to note that European Jews would often raise money by auctioning the opportunity to have an *aliyah* (which was considered an honor). In this case, the sexton would be the auctioneer for each *aliyah*; once the *aliyah* was purchased, it could either be used for oneself or given away as a gift.

Finally, Samuel gets a job delivering meat for a butcher. Samuel felt humiliated working for someone else, but he indicates "need breaks iron." This is a common theme throughout the diary. Samuel, once strong, has now been broken. He is the "wounded hero" who has now fallen.

I (Paul Abramson) have a number of reactions to this section. First, it surprised me that Samuel lied about my father's academic career. A diary is presumably the place to express hidden feelings. I guess I would have expected Samuel to have stated something like: "Leonard flunked out of college. I feel hurt and upset, and worry about his future. Perhaps I am partly to blame. . . . " Instead, Samuel lied (or was psychologically incapable of discerning the truth), which makes me question the strength of his integrity. Thus, even if this diary was written for posterity, I do not understand why he disguised this circumstance. Perhaps I do not appreciate the significance of this event, and therefore, underestimate the desire to correct the truth. On the other hand, maybe Samuel was like the Irish proverb, "It is a deaf person who lies." Certainly, it was the case that he couldn't "hear" the culpability of others, which was combined with his narcissism and a strong need to blame himself.

* * *

In July 1938, with God's help, I opened a liquor store. It wasn't easy to raise the money, but my brother-in-law, Abe Slavitt, cosigned a loan for me, for $600.

The business was quite good. My son helped to stock and organize the store. And after 6 months, the store began earning a living.

God is better than all—one should not lose hope. No one knows what time will bring.

I was overjoyed to be in business again for myself. And with God's help, I hope I'll continue to earn a good living there.

The winter of 1939 was a bit difficult. Business declined, but with God's help, we'll pull through.

In March of 1939 my brother-in-law, Abe Slavitt, had an operation to remove some gallstones. He was in the hospital for 2 weeks, and thank God, he has fully recovered.

On April 18, 1939, I didn't feel well. I went to Dr. Rosenthal, and he told me I had a weak heart. But even before I went to him, I knew that it was true. How can one have a healthy heart when one has so much worry and heartache?

I've had very little pleasure in my life. In a way, I'm angry: I've worked my entire life, and would hate to have to die penniless. No insurance, and no home. All gone by the wayside. And struggled all my adult life, and have nothing to show for it. But God will help.

Dr. Rosenthal took me to Dr. Yohn, who discovered that I have diabetes. I weighed too much (207 lbs.) for my height (5'7"), so I was put on a strict diet.

In May of 1939, I went back to Dr. Yohn. I stopped eating sugar, and my weight went down. I even feel considerably better. Also, I know God will help, if I take further care of myself, which I'll do.

God is ever-present in Samuel's life. Samuel gives thanks to God ("and thank God"), his success is dependent upon God ("with God's help"), he praises God ("God is better than all"), and he makes assurances for God ("I know God will help"). Moreover, he invokes the name of God in the three specific areas of family, health, and business.

Why the current preoccupation with God? The diary suggests two possibilities. First, Samuel is bitter and disillusioned ("I've had very little pleasure in my life"). Second, Samuel's health is failing. He is 54 years old, and has been diagnosed as having a "weak heart," as being obese (207 lbs at 5'7"), and as having diabetes. Thus, Samuel is confronting his mortality, and assessing the meaning of his existence. In neither case is Samuel happy. He believes that he has failed, and that time is running out.

How does Samuel cope? He has two strategies. First, he adopts an obsessive preoccupation with money and business. Presumably, this enhances his feelings of control, and binds his anxiety into a concrete problem. Second, he invokes the name of God. Besides assuaging his fears about death, perhaps Samuel's faith helps to minimize his self-blame. For instance, if Samuel is part of a larger plan that is beyond his grasp and understanding, then perhaps he is not entirely culpable for his failures.

Why is Samuel so bitter and disillusioned? Did life pass him by? Did he miss his chance? Perhaps, as we have suggested, the return on his investment (i.e., emigration) was never realized, and instead, he has spent much of his life accommodating to the trials and tribulations of establishing oneself in an adopted homeland. Of course, his childhood was probably not optimal—nor was that of his parents—so his foundation may also have been weak. Consider the following: He grew up in an impoverished and unstable country. His people were persecuted and sometimes slaughtered for their religious beliefs. His family lacked intimacy and affection. He left home, at 18 years of age, and traveled across a great ocean. He couldn't speak English. He worked as a peddler. He was lonely and isolated. And so on. Thus, in many ways it is hardly surprising that Samuel feels disillusioned, that he is plagued by anxiety and depression, and that he has been unable to summon his resources to combat his inner turmoil. Certainly, he had much to contend with.

*   *   *

Business slumped during the last week of May. Also, I sent for my liquor license, but it was hard for me to raise the money to pay for it. So, I had to take out a bank loan. But with God's help, I'll pay it off.

In July of 1939 I received the liquor license, thank God. Unfortunately, business was slow, but we are used to struggling. And anything is better than working for someone else.

My dear daughter (Sylvia) met a fine young man from New York, through my sister Esther. He appealed to us very much, and things look good. My daughter went to New York to meet his family.

However, now it seems that nothing will materialize. He was not what we thought he was. It is my deepest hope that my child should meet a fine, intelligent, and educated young man. Riches are good, but education is better. Money can disappear, but education lasts forever.

It's September of 1939. War has broken out in Europe. Germany attacked Poland. And France and England declared war on Germany. On September 18, Russia enters Poland.

It's December 1939, and bills have accumulated. I owed $300, and was blacklisted. This gave me much worry. So, I took out a $350 loan from the bank, and will work it out.

Business is still about the same. Also, there were new elections at my lodge, and Mr. Lupafsky was elected shamash, instead of me. I know I was a good and faithful worker, but it wasn't appreciated.

It's March 1940. My dear son Leonard completed several good business deals, and earned a nice few dollars. He affords me much pleasure, and I hope to God that he'll work his way up. He already has $600 from these transactions.

Mr. Novorky and Morris Voges died in May 1940. Mr. Becker also died.

It's June 1940. Italy has joined in the war, and Germany is now 35 miles from Paris.

A very fine young man came to Pesach, in South Norwalk. His name is Rabbi Tumin.

On June 10, the Germans entered Paris. It looks very bad. Also, America wants to send help to England.

On June 25, France surrendered to Germany. Now, we must wait and see what comes next.

On June 24, I sent away for the new liquor license. Thank God, business is not bad, and I hope it'll get better. The money for the license was taken out of the business, even though it was a little rough. However, I believe it isn't too late for things to pick up.

In June, Rabbi Tumin was installed as our new Rabbi. His installation was held at the Jewish Center. There were excellent speakers, and a marvelous supper. Mr. Nevis and Mr. Slavitt organized the affair.

On July 30, 1940, we moved to Elmwood Avenue. For the past 3 years, we'd lived at 15 Lowe Street, but had a very bad landlord. Finally, we'd had enough, and decided to move. But, we hope to God that we won't have to move again, because this wasn't an easy task.

Business wasn't bad. Also, my dear son made several more business deals, and my dear daughter is very pleased with our new home.

On October 16 the Draft Bill was passed. God should help, that my dear son won't be affected by it. Also, the news indicates that the Jewish situation throughout the world is now very bad.

On October 29, 1940, draftees' numbers were called. My son's number was 430. Thank God, he wasn't selected for induction.

Italy attacked Greece. Also, the presidential elections are coming up. President Roosevelt is running, for a third term, against Wendell Wilkie.

However, thank God, on November 6, 1940, President Roosevelt was reelected by a large majority. Now, we hope that times will get better. One has to hope for better times.

It's November of 1940. We enjoyed ourselves very much at our Thanksgiving dinner. Only our family attended. And I beg of you, dear God, that next year my dear daughter should be married. That is my deepest hope.

Samuel's "deepest hope" is that his daughter will get married. Parents often have fantasies about the marriage of their children, though not usually a "deepest hope." Instead, health and happiness take priority over marital designs. However, as far as Samuel was concerned, Sylvia's well-being was dependent upon a prosperous marriage.

Samuel defined a suitable groom as "a fine, intelligent, and educated young man." Presumably, by "education," Samuel meant a professional degree. Furthermore, Samuel states his preference for education over money: "Money can disappear, but education lasts forever".

Does education last "forever"? While a professional degree is not rescindable, continued prosperity is dependent upon the person, not the degree. However, having the degree provides a wider range of opportunities, and greater status. And in this respect, it often lasts "forever."

But Samuel may have had a more personal interest in "forever." He was getting older, his health was failing, and he was depressed. Thus, if his daughter can find "long lasting happiness" through a prosperous marriage, then future generations will have greater stability. Also, since Samuel was depressed, he probably wanted Sylvia (who was now 26) off his hands. Hence, even though Sylvia was employed as a teacher, she was still part of Samuel's burden, that is, the unmarried daughter. Therefore, if Sylvia would form a profitable marriage, it would have the dual consequence of lessening Samuel's load, and facilitating the future of the Abramson dreams.

It is interesting to note that Samuel is finally discussing both of his children in affectionate terms. Sylvia is a "dear, lovely" daughter, and "dear" Leonard (who is approximately 24 years old) "affords me much pleasure." Perhaps, as wage-earning young adults, Leonard and Sylvia have now grown in esteem. On the other hand, it is also probable that Samuel's sense of mortality, and the impending world crisis, have facilitated his appreciation of the intimate, familial pleasures of life. Note his enjoyment of the Thanksgiving dinner.

Besides his interest in business, Samuel is clearly preoccupied with world events. Community interests have expanded to the broader arena of the world as the major powers prepare for global war. The jeopardy of the Jews, and a son of draftable age, have obviously heightened his concerns.

It is surprising that Samuel did not express more personal reactions about Russia ("Russia enters Poland"). Did he sever all emotional ties to the country of his birth? Or, after 37 years, is it a matter of "out of sight, out of mind"?

Finally, Samuel continues to remain active in local Jewish affairs. He is bitter about losing an election, but is enjoying the new Rabbi. In fact, Samuel's scrapbook contains one of Rabbi Tumin's speeches. Delivered on Christmas to the Beth Israel Conservative Congregation, Rabbi Tumin's speech urged both Jews and Christians to unite for world peace. In this thoughtful sermon, Rabbi Tumin states, "In contemplating the ideals of peace and tolerance which this period represents, one's attention is inevitably drawn to a consideration of the world in which we live. As we look about us, what spectacle do we behold? We find a world, still writhing in the agonies of open wounds of the last great debacle, already engaged in another cataclysm of such vast proportions that upon its outcome will depend the crucial question of whether civilization itself is to survive . . . (and) on the eve of the Christmas celebration, Norwalk Jewry clasps hands with Christian friends and together pray for the realization of that day when 'nation shall not lift up sword against nation, neither shall they learn war any more.' . . . "

Why did Samuel include this speech in his scrapbook? Why was it significant? Was it Rabbi Tumin's only speech? Or did it have special meaning to Samuel? The prospect of world peace was certainly relevant to Samuel's concerns. But what about the unity of Christians and Jews?

Evidence suggests that Samuel was "color blind." For instance, in 1928, his son's scoutmaster was black (see p. 168). Also, Samuel was very active in a variety of ethnic celebrations. Finally, as a volunteer firefighter and police officer, he was a rarity as a Jew. Thus perhaps Samuel's vision of the world included the protection and safety of the Jews, in conjunction with the protection and safety of all people.

*   *   *

Business was very good, thank God.

On November 22, 1940, I turned 56 years old. I was born on the 21st day of Cheshvan, and I pray to God, that He should fulfill my desires, while I'm still alive.

I had previously borrowed $300 from the bank, and now have paid it off. At present, my outstanding debts are only $200. Times are getting better.

Mussolini is being "paid" back. Churchill spoke, demanding that the Italian people overthrow him. However, battles are still going on.

On December 27, 1940, my dear daughter met a fine young man from Bridgeport. We hope that something serious will develop.

Unfortunately, nothing happened. However, I'm sure that God will send her the husband He intended.

Our remaining debt, thank God, was finally paid off.

It's February 1941. The European battles are still going on. Also, President Roosevelt implored Congress to appropriate assistance for England. Unfortunately, he's had much difficulty. However, it's hoped that this bill will pass.

In the meantime, things don't look good. Business isn't bad (I do about several hundred dollars a month now), but cash is scarce. And this is hard for me. I worry every day, but one must hope for better times. However, anything is better than working for someone else.

On March 10, 1941, Roosevelt signed the Lend Lease Bill. He requested $7 billion from Congress, to help rid the world of dictators.

The Jewish people are suffering more than anyone. We hope that there'll be a quick end to the war. And that England will drive Italy out of Ethiopia, allowing Haile Selassie to again become king.

It's April 17, 1941, and the war continues. Germany went into Czechoslovakia.

We have now passed the Lend-Lease Bill. May it not be too late. America is trying her best.

This Pesach, Sylvia took a trip to Johnstown, Pennsylvania, for a vacation. Also, Leonard has moved out of Abe Slavitt's office (which he shared), because they didn't get along.

Business has improved, thank God.

Rabbi Tumin was again elected as Rabbi, with a raise of $1,000. He now receives $4,000 a year. He's a fine man and a very good person.

Greece surrendered to the powerful Germans. Now, America must help England. Only God knows how this will end.

The land of Palestine may be in deep trouble because Germany wants Iraq's oil—which leads to the Haifa pipeline. If it comes to a German invasion of Palestine, the Jewish people will have horrible times.

It's April 20, 1941, and Leonard is trying to establish an office for himself. It's a false world. Each person only looks out for himself. Who cares about another?

Dr. Clarence Abramson had an operation. He feels better, but he isn't receiving any of his patients. Also, on May 10, 1941, my son Leonard badly twisted his foot. It took a month before he could walk again. Thank God, Dr. Abramson was able to take care of him.

On June 23, 1941, I sent away for my fourth liquor license. Business is better, it has doubled. And it stays busy. I made $300 a week.

Germany declared war on Russia. And England has bombed Germany more and more.

On June 28, 1941, Bobby Slavitt became engaged. There were 300 people invited to the shul, and it was a beautiful and very elegant party. Everyone was impressed. Also, my cousin Yechiel, and his wife and children, visited me.

I received my new liquor license. Business is better and better—more than $300 a week. I hope to God I'll be able to save a few dollars for when I can't work. I already feel that age is creeping up on me. And I hope to God that I'll be able to provide for us. And furthermore, that we won't have to go to the children for help.

I started purchasing liberty bonds in the name of my wife. She has certainly earned it.

As noted earlier, Robert Abramson (Samuel's father) died at the age of 58. And now, Samuel is 56 years old. Samuel is anxious and bitter, and fears that "age is creeping up on" him. Are these concerns escalated by thoughts about his father? Will Samuel share his father's fate and die at 58? Or will Samuel be "reprieved"?

Additionally, it appears that Samuel continues to fear dependency ("anything is better than working for someone else"). Furthermore, regardless of the solvency of his business, he worries every day. And how does Samuel manage these obsessional fears? He appeals to God.

While praying to God is certainly an integral part of one's relationship with God, the relationship need not be restricted to divine appeals. However, in Samuel's case, it appears that his spirituality is limited to expectations for divine intervention on a material level. Absent from this diary are expressions related to spiritual guidance, ethical debates, or metaphysical concerns. Moreover, except for Jewish holidays, there is no mention of love, or appreciation of the Torah or Jewish ritual. While Samuel certainly embodies many humanitarian ideals, the diary suggests that his reference to God is limited to pragmatic concerns.

One pragmatic concern is the marriage of his daughter. Samuel indicates that "God will send the husband He intended." Presumably, Samuel's expectation is related to the Jewish belief that God selects, prior to birth, a future spouse for every infant. For instance, there is a *midrash* (a rabbinic homily), which states that 40 days prior to the birth, a *bat kol* (the voice of an angel) calls out "this baby so and so will marry such and such." Thus, all marriages are assumed to be preordained and "made in heaven." A similar belief is also expressed in another Jewish homily (or *midrash*). According to this story, a very prominent Roman matron summoned a famous rabbi to her home. Point-blank, the matron asked the rabbi, "What does the Jewish God do all day?" The rabbi replied, "He decrees matches in marriage." The matron scoffed at the "idiocy" of this task, and vowed to demonstrate that marriage did not require divine intervention. For instance, that evening she married 1,000 of her male servants to 1,000 of her female servants. When done, the matron stated, "That was simple." However, the following morning, all was not well. Many of her servants were bruised, some were blinded, and others had broken limbs. Furthermore, all the servants demanded to be separated from their partners. At this point, the matron turned to the rabbi and said, "Indeed, the Jewish people have a very great and mighty God" (Bereishit Rabba 68:2).

In addition to his preoccupations with business and marriage, Samuel was also concerned with the politics of his day. As mentioned earlier, the progress of the war was of vital interest. Furthermore, the status of the Jews and the fate of Palestine were relevant to his religious and ethnic identity as well as his Zionist beliefs. Finally, it also appears that Samuel had a particular interest in Haile Selassie of Ethiopia (who was dethroned by Mussolini's army). Although Selassie was black (a purported descendant of King Solomon and the Queen of Sheba), and ruled a predominantly black country, Americans were sympathetic to his plight because he fought against the allies of

Germany. Furthermore, when exiled, Selassie resided in Jerusalem, thereby establishing a further connection with the Jews. Thus, not surprisingly, Samuel was drawn to Selassie. He hopes that "England will drive Italy out of Ethiopia, allowing Haile Selassie to again become king." Notice that Samuel is not interested in British rule of Ethiopia, but instead, prefers the rightful heir. Moreover, since Ethiopia encompassed the Falashas Jews (who are black), Samuel probably had an additional "connection" to this country. In either case, it once again suggests that Samuel was "color blind."

Samuel also indicates that "Germany wants Iraq's oil." This comment is in reference to the British-owned Iraqi Oil Company. Prior to World War II, oil flowed from Iraq, through Palestine, to the port of Haifa, the site of British refineries. Obviously, during World War II, the British navy was highly dependent upon this oil. Thus, if Hitler had successfully bombed (or captured) this pipeline, it would have had dire consequences for the British navy, as well as the Jews in Palestine.

Finally, Samuel mentions that he purchased liberty bonds in his wife's name. Samuel affirms "she has certainly earned it." However, if she has "earned" it, why did it take so long (he was 56 years old) to "pay" her? Furthermore, since when does a spouse "earn" his or her keep? Was their relationship based upon reciprocal obligations? Were "rewards" given for long-term service? If so, what about love, intimacy, and affection?

*   *   *

On July 11, 1941, Leonard received the draft questionnaire. He filled it out, and we shall see how he did.

On July 17, 1941, Leonard made a few good business deals. He paid his debts and accumulated $235, which he gave to Sylvia. In a second deal, he made $112—thank God—and also stands to make $400 if he sells his stock.

It's July 20, 1941. Three years ago, my son met a girl from New Canaan, Connecticut. We found her very lovely. I also knew her parents (very fine people). However, now he met another girl who appealed to him. We will see what materializes. I must say that I was annoyed that he disappointed the girl from New Canaan. Evidently, he dropped her. Let's see if anything will happen with the new girl.

Leonard went to the Draft Board to be examined. We hope he'll be deferred.

Fortunately, Leonard was deferred until after Christmas. What'll happen remains to be seen.

Leonard bought a dog, a dalmatian. We named it Rex, after a previous dog. The first dog was only 8 weeks old when we got him. We loved him, but he got sick and died. We hope this dog will live longer.

In March of 1941 Leonard became acquainted with Dorothy Safir, who lives next door to us. She'd visited him when he was laid up with his bad ankle. Now they're going out together. It remains to be seen what will develop.

On December 14, 1941, my son, with God's help, is getting married to Dorothy Safir.

On November 3, 1941, I paid off the loan of $300, which I borrowed from Abe Slavitt. Everything is getting dearer. I now make about $300 a week.

The government just put a $4 tax on each case of liquor.

The war is still going on. Russia is putting up a stiff fight against Germany. What will happen remains to be seen.

On November 11, 1941, I turned 57 years old, thank God. Business is good, and life shouldn't be any worse than it is now.

My son Leonard and his sweetheart went to Baltimore to get married. But the rabbi refused to marry them because he didn't know the family, and so on. So they came home and told us of their plans. It was a surprise to us, since Leonard still has to hear the final word from the Draft Board. But we are very happy. It's my hope to live and see my son married. Thank God his bride is a very fine person, and we are both very happy with her.

On December 5, 1941, our children went to New York, with Rabbi Tumin, to arrange for their wedding. They took a blood test there. Perhaps if they had been married in Baltimore, things would have been simpler for them. But we would not have had the pleasure of escorting him to the altar. The wedding will be December 14, with mazel ("luck").

In the meantime, Japan attacked the United States. And we have declared war on Japan. One of Dorothy's brothers was in Honolulu at the time, and her mother is very worried. She has not heard from him.

The President called Congress into session, and declared war against Japan. I hope this will not affect the wedding, and that it will occur as planned.

On December 11, 1941, Italy and Germany declared war on America.

Leonard got his marriage license and the wedding will be Sunday, with mazel ("luck"). It will not be a large wedding. Only close family will attend, and Rabbi Tumin will officiate.

I, and my wife Esther, think Dorothy is a very lovely child. And we think, with God's help, that our son will be very happy with her. When Leonard marries, I'll try my best to help him with as much as I am able. Just let it be with mazel ("luck").

On December 13, 1941, I had a little trouble with my family. Some of them were insulted that they weren't invited to the wedding. I told them that the bride's mother wanted a very private affair. Dorothy's brother was in the Philippines, with the Army, and as such, we didn't want to make a big wedding. Fortunately, we straightened everything out.

On Sunday morning, as we were leaving for the wedding, a telegram arrived. It was from the bride's brother, in Honolulu, saying that he was okay.

It's December 14, 1941. This Chanukah eve was one of the happiest moments of my life. I led my son to the marriage canopy. Our whole immediate family was there—my mother (who rose from a sickbed), Rachel and her husband, Jennie and her husband, and Esther and her husband. The wedding was in the Waldorf-Astoria in room 1079. Rabbi Tumin officiated, and I read the marriage contract. After the ceremony, drinks and refreshments were served. Then we left for Siegel's Restaurant, had a very good dinner and a swell time. Everything was kosher, and in the best of taste. My dear daughter was the maid of honor, and Dr. Clarence Abramson was the best man. My son looked very handsome, and his bride lovely. We wish them many good and happy years. May God allow them to live out their lives in peace. That is what I, and my dear wife, wish them. God knows we deserve this naches ("favor"), for all the hardships we've endured. We thank God for everything. Now, we also wish that we'll live to escort our dearly beloved daughter to the marriage canopy.

It's December 15, 1941. The Norwalk papers found out about our son's marriage, and printed an announcement. It was a pleasant surprise. And as a result of the article, we received many well wishes for the newlyweds.

Also, The New York Times mentioned the wedding, and the young couple sent out announcement cards to one and all.

My sister Jennie made them a kitchen shower, and they received many gifts.

Leonard rented a house on Silver Street. We'll see what will happen with the Draft Board and his military service.

Leonard received nearly $1,000 in wedding presents.

For New Year's, my wife and I visited our children. I was very pleased to see my son and his wife in their own home, which is very nicely furnished. I hope that God will give them many happy years. May they live and be well.

In December business was good. I took in $1,750. Now I hope that I'll be able to accumulate a few dollars for my later years—because life without money is very bad.

On January 9, 1942, my sister had a bridal shower for my daughter-in-law. The whole family came and brought beautiful presents. May the couple enjoy them in good health. Also, I hope to God that I'll live to see this for my beloved daughter.

On January 11, 1942, I and my wife went to visit our dear children, the young couple. We pray that Leonard should make a good and easy living for himself and family.

It's January 12, 1942. This is the first time I met Sylvia's new boyfriend. I hope she'll marry him. He's a very fine, intelligent young man, just the kind she likes.

Her boyfriend is in the shoe business. My sister Jennie introduced him, through Mr. Gotfried.

My daughter is a very good soul. She always helped us in bad times. May God repay her with a good future.

On January 14, 1942, another linen shower was held for my daughter-in-law, by her Uncle Sol's family. Again, she received beautiful gifts and the best of everything. My wife and daughter attended. May she use them all in the best of health.

Leonard Abramson married Dorothy Safir on December 14, 1941. Samuel states that it was "one of the happiest moments of my life."

However, there is some confusion about this marriage. For instance, the diary indicates that Leonard was dating a girl from New Canaan for 3 years. She was "very lovely" and her parents were "very fine people." Nevertheless, the relationship did not last. Leonard found someone else. Thus, on July 20, 1941, Samuel is "annoyed" that the New Canaan girl has been "disappointed," but is also guardedly optimistic about the "new girl."

Who was the "new girl"? Was she Dorothy Safir? And if so, why isn't she mentioned by name. Samuel knew Dorothy (and her parents); they were next-door neighbors. Instead, Dorothy is mentioned in November, out of chronological order, as becoming "acquainted" with Leonard in March 1941, when Leonard was bedridden with a bad ankle. Now "they are going out together" (November 1941), and plan on "getting married" (December 1941).

Why the rush? And why did they attempt to elope to Baltimore? As Samuel indicates, the rabbi in Maryland refused to marry them. Presumably, Leonard and Dorothy were unable to substantiate their Jewish parentage. For instance, when a rabbi requires proof of Jewish heritage, copies of both parents' *ketubas* (the Jewish wedding document) are usually required. As an alternative, the couple is entitled to have two kosher witnesses who are present and swear to the following: (a) that they know the parents of the bride and groom; and (b) that the parents are Jewish. (An accompanying call to the parents' rabbi may also be necessary.) Since Leonard and Dorothy were unprepared for either alternative, the Baltimore plans were undoubtedly impulsive.

Why Baltimore? And why not Connecticut? Was Dorothy underage? Did she need parental consent? Did the parents not approve?

As the diary indicates, Samuel was very pleased with the wedding and thought very highly of Dorothy. Yet, there are no qualitative comments about Dorothy's parents. Did he like them or not? And what were *their* feelings?

Despite the impending war, Samuel took great pride in the wedding. He enjoyed leading his son to the "marriage canopy." This canopy, known as a *huppah,* consists of a cloth (often a *tallis* or prayer shawl) that is spread on poles and held over the bride and groom. The *huppah* is symbolic of the house the couple will now build together. Samuel also mentions that he read the marriage contract. Called the *ketuba,* the marriage contract is written in Aramaic, and it records the husband's financial obligations. The *ketuba* was originally instituted to make it more difficult for a husband to divorce his wife.

Although the wedding was a "very private affair," it was undoubtedly glamorous, that is, held at the Waldorf-Astoria, and noted in *The New York Times.* The reception also appears to have been festive. Held at Siegel's Restaurant, it was entirely kosher. "Kosher," by the way, refers to one of the main tenets of *Koshrus.* This tenet prohibits eating (or cooking) dairy products and meat dishes together. Therefore, kosher restaurants serve either a dairy menu or a meat menu, but not both. Siegel's, which is still in business in New York City, is a non-dairy restaurant. Perhaps, there were no kosher restaurants in Norwalk, and thus eating at Siegel's was a novelty.

It is interesting how quickly Samuel "adopted" Dorothy. After the marriage, the bride and groom became "our dear children, the young couple." Besides being happy about the marriage (and the many gifts), Samuel was also enjoying his increased financial stability (i.e., "everything getting dearer"). Thus, he now appears sensitive to Leonard's happiness ("God give them many happy years"), as well as his prosperity ("good and easy living").

Finally, Samuel continues to pray for his daughter. She is "a very good soul . . . (who) has helped us in bad times." Presumably, the prayers are devoted to Sylvia's prospects for marriage.

*   *   *

It's February 2, 1942. The Draft Board called my son in again for an eye exam. It remains to be seen how he made out. Let us hope for the best.

My daughter is still going out with her friend. We hope they will decide to get married. Time will tell. She has already visited his family in New York.

Leonard was notified by the local Draft Board that he is 1A and that he'll have to go to Hartford. Let us see what will happen.

On March 14, 1942, Leonard enlisted in the army, and he is waiting to be called. I pray to God that everything will be all right. It's very difficult for me to get accustomed to this idea. But what can one do? Such is life.

On March 27, 1942, Leonard was informed by the Draft Board that he reports on April 1. But this date is eruv Pesech, and we hope that he can remain with us for these few days. In the meantime, he's giving up his house. And when he leaves, his wife will return to stay with her parents.

It's April 1, 1942. Leonard was with us for Pesech seder. Dorothy, Sylvia and her friend, my mother, and my sister (and her family) were also present. My dear wife prepared a splendid meal—the best of everything. Dear God, keep us together, and let us meet again next year, in peace.

On April 2, 1942, Leonard left for Stamford, Connecticut. May God bring him back to us the same as he left us. Sylvia and Esther, the Slavitts, Uncle Leventhal, and Rachel were at the train, at 7:30 in the morning, to see him off.

We heard from Leonard immediately upon his arrival. God should keep him safe and return him to us.

It's April 9, 1942. We received letters and telephone calls from Leonard. In the meantime, he's at Camp Devons, Massachusetts.

Lately, Leonard's mother and I often review our past. We think of the sacrifices we made to bring up our children— with all the advantages—only to have our son in the army. This makes us sorrowful. But what can we do? I pray he'll come back well.

On April 9, 1942, we received a letter from Leonard. He's being sent to South Carolina. Now, we are waiting for another letter from him.

It's April 13, 1942. Thank God he has arrived in South Carolina: Company C, 38th Infantry Boot Camp Croft, Platoon #4. Let him only be well.

On April 25, 1942, we received good letters from Leonard. He wrote us that his wife is pregnant. We are very happy to hear this. And we pray to God that all will end well. That is our dearest wish.

Mrs. Safir and my daughter-in-law are mad at us. We don't know why. She doesn't visit us, which hurts us. God knows we are not guilty of any wrongdoing, and we are delighted that our daughter-in-law is pregnant.

It's May 1942. Today it is 6 weeks since Leonard was inducted into the army and left for Camp Croft. Let us hope for peace in the world. And that Leonard should return to us soon, well and healthy. That is our whole hope.

Three months after the wedding, Leonard enlisted in the army. He was classified as 1A, and presumably would have been drafted in short order. Samuel accepts the military obligation with fatalistic resignation, that is, "such is life."

However, after Leonard has departed, Samuel's feelings are more pronounced. He is bitter and disillusioned: (thinking) "of the sacrifices we made to bring up our children—with all the advantages—only to have our son in the army. This makes us sorrowful. But what can one do? I pray he'll come back well."

Samuel's pain and sadness are certainly evident in this segment of the diary. Samuel is facing a very difficult time and is trying his best to cope with these circumstances. Not surprisingly, his method of coping reflects his general perspective on life. For instance, he indicates that, "we worked so hard, and now we get nothing." Did he really get nothing? What about the previous 25 years with Leonard? Were they without joy? Also, parents often "sacrifice" for their *own* needs and benefits. Furthermore, it is obvious that very few children get "all the advantages." Was this true of Leonard and Sylvia? Did they receive unconditional love and affection, as children, from both parents? Perhaps the diary suggests not. And finally, while Samuel's grief is understandable, he also seems to be presenting himself as a martyr—suffering pain and sacrifice, but coming up empty. If this is true, perhaps there is a hidden guilt: Samuel and Leonard have finally grown close. But now, Leonard has been taken away. And as a consequence, Samuel is grieving over the loss *and* the time misspent.

Prior to leaving, Leonard and Dorothy attended a Passover dinner. Many relatives were present, except, notably, Dorothy's parents. Shortly thereafter, Dorothy announced that she was pregnant, and the Safirs (including Dorothy) ceased contact with Samuel and his wife. Samuel was hurt, and lamented, "God knows we are not guilty of any wrongdoing."

What happened? Pregnancy is usually a time of celebration. Was it Samuel? Was it Leonard? Or the marriage?

Finally, there is a distinct change in Samuel's prayers. They have depth and meaning. And are clearly from the heart. For instance: "Dear God, keep us together, and let us meet again next year, in peace." Unlike his previous prayers, this anthem has meaning for every family in crisis, regardless of time, place, or religion.

*　　*　　*

It's May 22, 1942. Leonard is now in Officers Training School. Let's hope he'll do well.

It is now Shavuos—7 weeks since Leonard went into the army.

My brother-in-law, Abe Slavitt, caused some trouble for my mother. Consequently, my sister Rachel has had to take our mother into her home. It seems like it doesn't pay to get old.

On July 10, 1942, I received a letter from Leonard, indicating that he's being sent away. Only God knows where. When he comes home on furlough, he'll let us know.

In the meanwhile, time flies. Business isn't bad. The week of July 4, I took in $431. Also, on June 23, I sent away for my liquor license. I paid for it out of my own money, not borrowed money.

Now, I plan to save a dollar a day. It's too difficult to come up with a large sum of money all at once.

Lastly, may we be healthy, and make a decent living.

My daughter-in-law, Dorothy, may she be well, got mad at us and doesn't come to visit anymore. This hurts and pains us very much. But what can I do? When she gets older, she'll surely understand how unjust she is to us. Leonard, on the other hand, can't help much. Five months have passed since he went away. But, I hope to God that all will straighten itself out in due time. Time heals all wounds.

It's July 22, 1942. During the summer, my dear daughter works in Bridgeport, for an ammunition firm. She is very patriotic. She earns a nice salary while on vacation from her teaching job.

Business has become very good. We make about $400 a week. In fact, business couldn't be better. Now, I hope to God, to be able to save some money for my old age. It's very sad to have to approach others for help, even if they are your own children. It seems the world stands on money. Life is very bitter without it.

We receive frequent letters from Leonard. I pray to God he'll do well in everything. Unfortunately, we haven't seen him for 5 months, since he's been at Camp Croft in South Carolina. Now, he's taking up typing and shorthand. These skills will come in handy some day.

It's hard for us to overcome our longing for our dear son.

It's Friday, July 31, 1942. My son's wife gave birth to a daughter, may she be blessed with a long life. Her name is Judith Ellen—Yehudis Chana. I bought a $25 Liberty Bond for her.

However, we haven't seen our grandchild yet. Her mother is playing politics with us. But we hope it'll blow over soon.

Mother and child feel fine.

Leonard hasn't come home on furlough yet.

It's August 14, 1942. Leonard still hasn't been able to come home to see his child. I feel for his unhappiness. But what can one do? The war has brought this to be.

God will repay Fannie, Leonard's mother-in-law, for not letting us see our first grandchild. It's very painful to have to bear this situation.

Also, it's very ugly. This behavior is fit for savages. Not for civilized people of today.

It always seems that one has to suffer. But I know, time will eventually heal all.

It's August 17, 1942. We were in Brooklyn for Soli's wedding and had a good time. And when we returned home, we were so surprised to find our dear son there. He'd received a 5-day pass to see his newborn daughter. And after seeing her, Leonard tells us that she is a very lovely child.

Words can't describe our delight, being together again with our child Leonard. Also, Dr. Clarence Abramson came from Brooklyn for a visit.

It's August 19, 1942. Leonard left today at 7 in the morning. May he go in good health and arrive in good health.

Originally, Leonard wrote that when he came home, he would take us to see his child. But in the meantime, Fannie (his mother-in-law) is the boss. Thus, we still haven't seen the child. And this pains and angers us, but what can we do?

It's August 24, 1942. We received a letter from Leonard. He's got an office job and he'll remain there until he's transferred. He has also signed up with the air corps.

It's August 29, 1942. We receive frequent letters from Leonard. He likes his new job. However, only God knows what the ultimate outcome will be. In the meantime, Leonard is satisfied.

Many young people are being sent to Europe. God help us, that our son will come out of this unharmed.

Meanwhile, we still haven't seen our grandchild. She's already one month old, but Fannie is still the boss. We suffer, and our heartache is great. And furthermore, we can't believe that this is happening in this century, not to be able to see the child.

I'll never forgive Fannie.

Leonard Abramson died on February 2, 1975. His obituary appeared in the Norwalk newspaper. It stated that Leonard Abramson was survived by his wife Ethel Sakowitz Abramson, and their four children, the eldest being Paul. Neither Dorothy Safir Abramson nor Judith Ellen Abramson was mentioned.

Prior to 1975 I (Paul Abramson) assumed (and was led to believe) that Ethel Abramson was my father's only wife. I was also told, by my entire family, that I was my father's first child. However, in 1975, through a chance event, I learned of his previous marriage.

This is how it happened. As the diary indicates, Leonard served in the armed services during the Second World War. As a veteran, he was entitled to service benefits. Thus, after his death, my mother completed a VA application. To my shock, in Background Information, my mother reported that my father was married previously, and had another child.

Since my mother was mourning, I didn't pursue my father's background until years later. However, I must admit that I was particularly fascinated with the diary sections dealing with Dorothy and Judith Abramson.

Judith Ellen Abramson was born on July 31, 1941, 7-1/2 months after Dorothy and Leonard Abramson were married. Presumably, the "aborted" Baltimore wedding and the hasty New York wedding were designed to disguise Dorothy's pregnancy. Thus, the confusion and the impulsive nature of their plans are now clearer.

Unfortunately, there was "trouble in paradise." Though neighbors, the in-laws stopped speaking, and Dorothy had refused to visit Samuel and his wife. Furthermore, when Leonard returned, it appeared that he stayed with his parents, and not with his wife and daughter.

What really happened? Did Dorothy tell her parents that she was pregnant? Did they blame Leonard and/or Samuel? Was there pressure to get married? And if so, was it for convenience, and presumed to be short-lived? Enough to give Judith legitimacy? Or did Dorothy and Leonard decide to get married on their own, and make the best of it? In either case, it is not a healthy start. Instead, it seems to have been a short-term affair, inexorably complicated by Dorothy's pregnancy. Furthermore, despite pretenses otherwise, it now appears to be falling apart.

Perhaps, Samuel was an unintentional victim in a charade. For instance, if the marriage was for appearance's sake only, there may have been an agreement to dissolve quietly. Except for Samuel, who genuinely cared for his daughter-in-law and granddaughter. On the other hand, maybe the marriage was meant to work. And instead, Leonard's induction into the army, and the prospect of World War II, undermined the shaky union. Furthermore, if the Safirs were not thrilled with the marriage in the first place, they may have facilitated the rift. Finally, it may have been Leonard's doing. For instance, if he was pressured into the marriage, his commitment to the armed services may have been a convenient way to withdraw. Unfortunately, the diary and family legend do not resolve this.

In either case, it appears that Samuel was genuinely hurt by this continuing soap opera. It was "painful," "ugly," and "uncivilized," and it reinforced Samuel's persistent theme that "one has to suffer." Furthermore, despite Dorothy and Leonard's culpability in this situation, Samuel blames Dorothy's mother ("I'll never forgive Fannie—for not being able to see the child").

Despite the family crisis, Samuel had a bright spot—his new prosperity. Business was very good (he was making between $1,600 and $2,000 per month), and Samuel enjoyed this newfound success. However, the novelty of a successful business did not eliminate Samuel's chronic insecurity ("It is very sad to have to approach others for help, even if they are your own children"). Samuel's dependency fears (or fears of intimacy) are perhaps also evident in his comments about his mother. Having "trouble" with Abe Slavitt, his mother relocates with his sister. Thus, Samuel concludes that "it doesn't pay to get old."

Samuel also eventually concludes that the "world stands on money." Presumably, this is Samuel's reinterpretation of a dictum in the *Sayings of the Sages* (Chapter 1, *Mishna* 2). Shimeon the Righteous, a member of the Great Assembly, who survived the destruction of the second Temple, used to say: "The world stands on three things: on Torah, on worship of God, and on the performance of acts of kindness." Perhaps Samuel equated money with the ability to act "kind." Thus, with less money, he may have convinced himself that his responsibilities were correspondingly less.

Finally, Samuel continues to long for his son. Seven weeks have passed, and it is now *Shavuos*. *Shavuos*, which is known as the Feast of Weeks, refers to the command in Leviticus (23: 15-16, 21) to celebrate the holiday 7 weeks after the first day of Passover. Orthodox Jews believe that *Shavuos* signifies the day that God gave the Torah to the Jewish people on Mount Sinai—7 weeks after the Exodus from Egypt. *Shavuos* is celebrated by an all-night vigil—studying the Torah and related subjects—to demonstrate one's enthusiasm and commitment to Torah. Also, according to Jewish law, writing is forbidden on *Shavuos*. However, on May 22, 1942, which is the first day of *Shavuos*, Samuel makes an entry in his diary. Thus, it is obvious that Samuel is not observing *Shavuos* according to the Orthodox tradition. Instead, it appears that he is a committed and religious Jew who celebrates Jewish holidays, but does not embrace the Orthodox perspective. Moreover, it also appears that Samuel uses Jewish holidays as "benchmarks" for significant life events, suggesting an intimate psychological connection between his life and his Jewish identity. In Samuel's mind, *Shavuos* and Passover signify Leonard's induction into the army—and the disruption of his family. And while Samuel takes pride in Leonard and Sylvia's patriotism, Leonard's absence is a painful loss.

One final note. For a diary to have any psychological significance it should be honest and forthright. And while it is clear that Samuel disguised certain facts (e.g., Leonard's academic career), the diary is also by no means sanitized. It has pain, misery, jealousy, pettiness, and so forth. Thus, in many ways, it appears to be an intimate record of Samuel's experiences and feelings.

However, I also want to stress that the diary is "lucky" to have survived. There is evidence that portions of the diary were destroyed. For example, all newspaper clippings and English references to Judith and Dorothy Abramson were removed (leaving old glue and empty spaces). Thus, it appears that someone (Samuel's survivors?) altered the record. Fortunately, however, the handwritten Yiddish was uncensored (by other family members), simply because no one else could read it. In this regard, the diary was protected by the ancient transcript.

Was it coincidental that Samuel wrote in Yiddish? Did he want the diary to survive? Did he want to keep the record straight? To provide "lessons" for future generations? Or did the diary represent his private thoughts, in his private language, that is, his "therapy"? Unfortunately, we'll never know. However, if fate is the judge, there appears to have been a purpose to the Yiddish disguise. Uncensored, the diary fell into the hands of a grandson, who was also a psychologist interested in case studies.

* * *

It's August 31, 1942. Sylvia has stopped working in Bridgeport. Thank God all is well.

Business has been very good this month. The store took in about $2,000. Thank God for all.

Finally, I have enough money to pay the bills.

My wife is now helping in the store. Consequently, I'm saving money to buy her a fur coat. And with God's help, she'll have it. She deserves it and has certainly earned it.

My good and devoted wife and I have gone through a hard life together. And now, I hope to God I'll be able to repay her for her devotion. May God give us good health, so that we can continue working and be able to overcome any further hardships. Amen, Amen.

It's September 2, 1942. My daughter and wife went shopping in New York. My wife took a good bit of money with her and bought three lovely dresses, plus a spring coat. I thank God for all of this. If one lives long enough, one will eventually live to see good. I'm very happy for my wife, because she had earned every bit of it.

On September 9, 1942, I purchased a $100 government bond. My total investment is now $400. May we continue to be well, and buy more.

We often receive letters from Leonard. He still has the office job, which is good. We hope that he returns to us in good health.

Business is good, thank God.

September 12, 1942, was Rosh Hashana. May this be a good year for all of us.

Services were held in Alex's Hall, and we were very satisfied. Everything went perfectly. And Rabbi Tumin's sermons were very good.

We received a record from Leonard and we were overjoyed to hear his voice. We also understand that his daughter is growing up very nicely. However, we have never seen her. God should pay her mother back for all our sorrow.

It's October 3, 1942. Six months have already passed since our beloved son Leonard went into the army. Now he has grown accustomed to it, and so have we. God gave us strength to endure our troubles, and overcome them.

Our granddaughter is now 2 months old, but we still haven't seen her. We pray that she is well, and is being raised properly by her mother.

Leonard hopes to get a short furlough to see the family. He is still at Camp Croft.

October 4, 1942, was Simchas Torah. Services were held at the Jewish Center.

The Conservative and Orthodox Jews don't see eye-to-eye. And I don't understand why there can't be peace between them here in Norwalk.

I was the bal tefilah for the morning and afternoon services. And afterwards, we had a very nice party. Everybody enjoyed it. And, please God, may we live to celebrate this again next year, and to have Leonard with us.

On October 12, 1942, I received a letter from Leonard. He passed the entrance exams for Officers Training School. I wish him good luck, and hope that he'll complete the course successfully.

Leonard writes that he expects to come home for a 10-day furlough. We're waiting impatiently for him. We miss him so much.

This situation is very hard to bear, but we can't do anything about it. That's life. And in life, many things occur over which we've no control—and don't like. But we must learn to put up with it. However, we're always hoping for better days.

It's October 15, 1942. Today at 2 p.m. I received a telegram from Leonard, asking me to send him $25. I immediately wired him the money, and it cost $1.30 to send it. Now, we're waiting impatiently for him to come. He received a 7-day furlough.

On October 16, at 2 A.M., Leonard arrived home. He had to travel 12 hours longer than usual. There were heavy rains, and he had to wait for another train. But thank God for everything.

Leonard looked fit. And now, he will be going to Texas, to study at the Officers Training School.

God should help us overcome all of this. We still haven't seen our grandchild. The mother-in-law dictates what goes on.

I gave Leonard $10 and Sylvia $5 for expenses on the way. May they leave in good health and arrive in good health. Amen, Amen.

On the morning of October 26, 1942, we received a telegram from Leonard, stating that he arrived safely at Fort Hood, Texas. May he always be well and be able to overcome all difficulties. And with God's help, come home in good health. Amen, Amen.

The liquor business received an additional $4.80 tax raise per gallon. Wine has also become more expensive. One must hope for better times. This week I earned $400. That's not bad—and I hope that it doesn't get any worse.

This month of October I took in $2,000, thank God. I also received a letter from Leonard. He writes that he's working 16 to 17 hours a day. He's very busy, and I hope to God that he'll succeed.

Today, I bought a war bond for $100. This comes to a total of $500 in war bonds.

On November 7, 1942, I received a letter from Leonard. He writes that he's working hard and that he hopes to come home in an officer's uniform. May God help him.

The Germans are on the run in Africa, and one hopes the war will soon be over.

Business is good, thank God.

Samuel appears obsessed with money: The world "stands on money," his diary is replete with concerns for money, and his personal relationships are described in monetary terms. For instance, Samuel wants to "repay" his wife for her devotion; Leonard "affords" him much pleasure; and Sylvia is a "good soul . . . may God repay her." However, despite what appears to be the neurotic nature of Samuel's obsessions, it should also be mentioned that "money" was a frequent metaphor in Yiddish idioms. Since daily sustenance was a critical preoccupation with most Jews in Eastern Europe, the Yiddish language was inundated with monetary references. For example, a Yiddish suggestion for relaxation might be: "Why not go and rest a little—it doesn't cost anything."

Despite his many worries, Samuel seemed to enjoy the Jewish holidays. *Rosh Hashana* signifies both the Jewish New Year and the Day of Judgment. As the New Year, *Rosh Hashana* commemorates the creation of the world and the initiation of the upcoming year. As the judgment day, *Rosh Hashana* also marks the time of evaluation. Positive and negative actions are weighed, and God is petitioned for inscription in the book of life (which, in turn, is sealed 10 days later on *Yom Kippur,* the day of atonement).

The most important ritual of *Rosh Hashana* is the blowing of the *shofar* (a hollow horn that can be drawn from any animal except a cow). Blowing the *shofar* is meant to awaken "unconscious" lapses in behavior, thereby recognizing God as creator and king, which, in turn, facilitates the process of repentance prior to *Yom Kippur.* Moreover, the traditional greeting for this day is *LeShana Tova Techasayvu VeTechataymu,* which means "May you be inscribed and sealed for a good year." Thus, Samuel concludes his thoughts about the holidays with "May this be a good year."

Samuel also indicates that *Rosh Hashana* services were held in "Alex's Hall." Obviously, Alex's Hall was not a temple, suggesting that his congregation did not have a synagogue. Furthermore, it appears that his congregation used several different facilities. For instance, *Simchas Torah* services were held at the Jewish Center (a large community center). *Simchas Torah* is the 8th day of *Sukkos* (the holiday of Booths), which follows 5 days after *Yom Kippur. Simchas Torah* literally means "rejoicing of the Torah." It signifies the completion of reading the Torah for one year, and the beginning of Torah reading for the new year. In both evening and daytime celebrations, all Torah scrolls are held by congregation members, who circle the *bimah* (pulpit) seven times, usually with dancing and singing.

Although Samuel takes pride in his Jewish identity, it also appears that he is bothered by the dissension in the Jewish ranks, that is, Conservative versus Orthodox. It should be noted that Conservative and Orthodox Judaism were more similar in the 1940s than they are today. Prior to the 1920s, the Conservative movement was primarily in opposition to the Reform movement. Thus, the early founders of Conservatism fully supported the observance of Orthodox traditions, rituals, and precepts. However, in contrast to the Orthodox perspective, the Conservatives believed that *halacha* (the Jewish legal code) was intended to be flexible, and as such was meant to be modernized. Moreover, by the 1940s, younger rabbis within the Conservative movement also petitioned to modernize Orthodox rituals. Therefore, within the Conservative community, there was dispute over the traditional versus innovative perspectives. And as a consequence, the innovations made it impossible for Conservative and Orthodox Jews to share ceremonies. Evidently, in Samuel's case, it appears that his Conservative group was displaced, since they observed services in a variety of facilities. Finally, Samuel indicates that he was the *Ba'al Tefilah,* literally the "master of prayer." In this capacity, Samuel led the congregation in prayer, suggesting that he received this honor because he knew the prayers, and he had a good voice.

Again, Samuel presents his world view ("many things occur over which we've no control . . . we must learn to put up with it"). Basically, he is stating that "life is miserable, but we hope for better days." This attitude (which may suggest chronic depression) is apparent throughout the diary. And while the antecedents of this perspective are obvious (i.e., the Russian Jewish experience and the impact of emigration), it is nonetheless a morbid outlook.

Finally, while Samuel concedes that he has grown used to Leonard's absence, his still sorely misses his son. Hearing the recording of Leonard's voice was clearly a thrill. Furthermore, both Samuel and Leonard seem optimistic about Officers Training School. On the other hand, Samuel is very pessimistic about his in-laws. Presumably, Dorothy and Leonard are still writing, since Leonard reports that Judy is doing fine. Last, in joint recognition of his prosperity and patriotism, Samuel has been actively purchasing war bonds.

*   *   *

It's November 14, 1942. We receive letters from Leonard every week. It takes 4 days for a letter to arrive.

Leonard hopes to pass his course. Also, he recently sent us the diploma he received upon becoming a corporal.

Now, his first period has ended. And with God's help, he passed. He wrote a letter to Sylvia explaining how difficult the school was. I hope that one day he will recall these times on joyous occasions.

It's November 18, 1942. We just sent a package of goodies to Leonard for Thanksgiving. Sylvia spent about $4 for the package, and I paid the 95¢ postage. May Leonard be well, and the time pass quickly.

Business is good. Stock is expensive. But we're all working.

The Allies are now in India. And at the gates of Tunis, attacking in Italy. With God's help, the war will come to a quick end.

It's November 25, 1942. Received a letter from Leonard. He's very busy, but with God's help, he hopes to successfully complete his courses.

The Allies appear to be winning the war. They're driving the Germans out.

Russia, the Americans, and the English have launched an invasion of Italy from Africa. With God's help, it appears to be going well. One hopes it won't be long. There must be an end to this war.

Business was good last month. October brought in $2,105.65. Thank God, I'm doing a bit better. I paid off the bills, and I've no more bank loans to pay, except one of Leonard's for $240.

I hope to God that I'll be able to help Leonard pay off his loan. And I hope to God that I'll never need any more: (a) bank loans; (b) approaching people to beg for a loan; or (c) finding someone to co-sign for my loans.

If one lives long enough, one will finally have better times. Blessed be God.

It's November 28, 1942. We had Thanksgiving dinner at home. It was a fine meal.

I hope to God that my family will again be together. And that we'll live to see peace in the world.

We receive frequent letters from Leonard. He's been studying for 5 weeks—out of a 13-week course. We hope he'll come home soon.

The French Navy wouldn't surrender. Instead, she sunk her ships rather than fall into Nazi hands.

Now it looks good. The American and English armies are on the outskirts of France.

It's December 9, 1942. We continue to receive mail from Leonard. He's working hard, but one hopes that he'll graduate soon. Seven weeks have passed, and only 6 weeks remain. We hope he'll make it. God help him. Amen, Amen.

It's December 14, 1942, one year since Leonard was married. Time has flown quickly, but much heartache has resulted. Leonard's wife and mother-in-law have yet to allow us to see the child.

Leonard has been in the army for 8 months. He's in Camp Hood, Texas, and will graduate in another 5 weeks. May God protect him, so that he remains healthy and comes back to his family. Time is a great healer.

Business is good. But it's a little hard to get merchandise, so one pushes on.

The battles are still continuing: The Allies are driving General Rommel (the German general) out of Africa; Mussolini is receiving plenty of heavy blows; and the Russians are driving the Germans back. But all this takes time, and I hope, with God's help, that the war will end soon. Amen, Amen.

Today, on December 23, 1942, we received a letter from Leonard. He didn't pass his exam. It was very hard, but he'll try again. One worries, but one hopes for better times.

I pray that the war will soon be over.

It's Christmas, and business isn't bad. But it's difficult to get goods. One hopes that things will improve.

It's December 28, 1942. We received a letter from Leonard, stating that he's in South Carolina, at Camp Croft. He's taking officer training again. We're waiting to see how he'll make out.

Last week we took in $521.08. This week, which included Christmas, I took in $715.17. I also gave a check of $160 to my wife Esther, toward her fur coat. I give her $5 a week for helping me. She has been with me in the store for one month. I hope to God she'll buy a good coat. She is worth it. She works hard.

During the month of December 1942, I took in a total of $2,389.37. My yearly income for 1942 was $20,454.99.

It's January 18, 1943. I received a phone call from Leonard, expressing that he's coming home for 9 days. We're awaiting his return, and we thank God for the acts of kindness that he bestows upon us.

Leonard came home on January 25, and finally brought our grandchild to visit us. I thank God that I lived to see my first grandchild. She is like a lovely little doll.

Unfortunately, his wife is still mad, but they'll straighten this out. It's not good for their child. And I pray to God that it'll all turn out for the best.

Leonard writes to his parents every week, chronicling his progress in Officers Training School. However, to his sister, he writes that OTS is very difficult. Why the discrepancy?

Obviously, Leonard's achievement record is not spectacular. He flunked out of college; his business prospects were unknown; and he failed Officers Training School. Thus, why the illusion? And furthermore, why the continued failure? Was college that hard? Was OTS that hard? Or was Leonard ill-suited for academic pursuit? If so, did he lack intelligence? Did he lack motivation? Or did he purposely undermine his chances?

Defeat is obviously difficult to admit. However, defeat can be softened by choosing an alternative route. Where Leonard is concerned, this was not the case. He pursued the academic track, without success. Why?

Samuel's business continues to rise. Although unable to appreciate his prosperity ("business isn't bad"—though he made more than $20,000 that year, which was a considerable amount for 1942), Samuel is certainly more optimistic. For instance, he hopes for the following: (a) Leonard will have fond memories of these times; (b) the war will end soon; (c) he won't need bank loans; and (d) Leonard's family crisis will be resolved.

Additionally, Samuel continues to express affection for Leonard. Obviously, Leonard's military service (during a war) would be a frightening prospect to any parent. Yet we wonder why Samuel was incapable of expressing equal affection, or concern (at least in the diary), prior to this circumstance. Perhaps Leonard's absence has "made the heart grow fonder"? If so, what inhibited the "heart" in the first place? Did fears of intimacy, or dependency, make this long-distance relationship more caring? Perhaps Samuel has great difficulty expressing either pride in himself or caring for others. As the diary suggests, he seems to measure happiness in terms of money. For example, Samuel's personal pride, or his pleasurable feelings, are often reported in dollars—sometimes in cents.

Finally, at long last, Samuel "lived to see his first grandchild"—many months after her birth. Obviously, something is very wrong. Surprisingly, however, the turmoil does not seem to have diminished Samuel's affection for Judy.

*　　*　　*

On the morning of January 27, 1943, Leonard left for South Carolina. I hope he'll complete his course.

President Roosevelt and Stalin met in Africa again, about the war. Thank God for all, and everything goes well. It's hoped that the war will now be over soon. However, the Jews of the world must offer a prayer and bensch gomel for the President, on his return from Casablanca.

It's February 23, 1943. We often receive letters from Leonard. He writes that he's continuing his officer training. I hope, with God's help, that he'll finish successfully this time.

Leonard's wife has stopped writing him. It troubles me very much that they don't agree. But I hope that, because of the child, they'll straighten out their differences.

Sylvia is going to visit Leonard, on February 27, for a week. May she go in good health and return in good health.

It's March 1, 1943. Sylvia has left to see Leonard in South Carolina. We received a telegram that she arrived safely, thank God, but her train was late. We're waiting for her to bring regards from him.

It's March 5, 1943. Goods are now difficult to obtain. But business is good, and we hope that it'll improve. In the meantime, it's hard to make ends meet. May God help end the war.

Germany is receiving plenty of blows from the air; Berlin was bombed, and Russia is driving the Germans back into their land.

Sylvia came home on March 8, 1943, at 3 P.M. She had a good time that week, and Leonard was very happy to have his sister with him. He's still in South Carolina. I thank God for all, and that he's still in the U.S.A.

Leonard is now finishing the course to become a 2nd lieutenant. However, his wife doesn't write him. Who knows what has happened between them? I'm very upset about this and I'm concerned for their beautiful child, who could be left to live as an orphan. It worries me very much, and this is not a happy time for me. It breaks my heart to see my son's life broken up.

On Friday, March 19, 1943, Mrs. Fischler died. Her funeral was Sunday in New York. She was buried in Mt. Zion Cemetery. She was 63 years old.

Samuel indicates that the "Jews of the world must offer a thanksgiving prayer for the President." In Yiddish, Samuel also suggested that Jews *bensch gomel* for the President. *Bensch* is a Yiddish word meaning "bless," and *gomel* is a Hebrew word meaning "deliverance." Jews invoke the "blessing of deliverance" when overcoming illness or danger (such as traveling). Moreover, the blessing is stated in front of the Torah, within the Synagogue. Thus, Samuel's suggestion that the Jews *bensch gomel* was requested for President Roosevelt following his return from Africa.

Since President Roosevelt was not Jewish, *bensching gomel* has an interesting symbolic meaning. Perhaps Samuel considered President Roosevelt Jewish in spirit (or sympathy) and, as such, warranted a Jewish blessing. On the other hand, Samuel may have also believed that God's blessings are not limited to Jews. For example, since the Jewish God is benevolent and farsighted, Samuel may have concluded that Jewish blessings are nondenominational, having relevance to everyone on earth. Finally, *bensching gomel* for President Roosevelt provides further evidence of Samuel's humanitarian spirit.

Leonard's marriage continues to descend. He and his wife are not corresponding, and Samuel is upset ("it breaks my heart"). However, it is not clear whether Leonard is equally distraught. No mention of Leonard's feelings is provided in the diary. Also, Samuel expresses the grave concern that Judy will become an "orphan." This is surprising, since neither parent is about to "die". Moreover, even in Jewish law (*halacha*), a child is not considered an orphan in the case of divorce. Consequently, this appears rather like hysteria (or perhaps involves borderline thinking), that is, grossly exaggerating the consequences of a disturbing situation. Furthermore, this irrational fear, is perhaps very close to an "unconscious wish." If Dorothy died, Leonard would have custody, and Samuel would have his granddaughter.

*   *   *

On March 23, 1943, we received a letter from Leonard. He passed his exams, and is continuing his officer's training. Also, I gave my beloved wife a check for $140. Now, she has $300 for a fur coat. It's well deserved. However, she is waiting for the April sales—and I hope she'll go to New York to buy herself a coat.

Business is about the same. Let us all be well.

It's April 3, 1943. Today, it's been a year since Leonard joined the army. May he be well and return home well.

I received a letter from Leonard. He writes that he's waiting to be sent to Fort Bragg, in Georgia, to finish his course. May he go in health and finish in health.

It's April 12, 1943. On Sunday, I received a telephone call from my wife's brother, that their father is very ill. And by Monday morning, when my wife left, he had already died. I wasn't at the funeral. It was too late to go.

We often receive letters from Leonard. He'll be in Officers Training School for another 2 weeks. Then, with God's help, he will have finished his schooling.

It's April 19, 1943, Passover eve. Business was good. Last week took in $542, the best the store has ever done. However, it's hard to get merchandise.

We received another letter from Leonard. I hope to God that next year he'll be with us at home.

It's April 27, 1943. I received a letter from Leonard. He has completed his 5th week of training for 2nd lieutenant. May God give us patience.

Business is good. Also, Abe Slavitt won the McCarthy case. It was a difficult lawsuit, but Abe was successful. Fortunately, Leonard will also get $500 from this case, which he'll use to cover the bank note that he took out before he left for the army.

Today, I went to services. I led the morning prayers and also the maftir. We hope that next year, God willing, Leonard will be with us.

Business is good, thank God. And during this month, I purchased three $75 war bonds. That comes to about $900 in war bonds.

It's May 7, 1943. My business brings in about $500 a week. Unfortunately, it's also hard to buy goods.

We received a letter from Leonard. An army commission appointed him to the Army College. We hope, with God's help, he'll complete this course.

It's May 8, 1943. I received an English Shas, plus a dictionary to help me use the Shas in good health. The dictionary is a present from Sylvia.

I received a telephone call from Leonard. He's coming home for a few days.

Leonard came home on May 10, at 2 P.M. He'll be here for several days.

Leonard has begun divorce proceedings. He can't live with his wife. Ultimately, he'll be better off. Dorothy had stopped writing him, which was the start of these troubles.

It pains me greatly! But how can I help? His child is very lovely. But who knows what will happen? We must wait and see. Time will tell.

On May 12, 1943, at 7 P.M., Leonard left. May he always be well. Also, he looks very good. And with God's help, all will pass successfully.

The Italians are on the run. One hopes for a quick end to the war.

Leonard paid off his bank loan with the money that he received from the McCarthy case. Thank God.

It's May 28, 1943. Leonard is still in South Carolina.

On May 27, 1943, the local newspaper reported that Leonard is divorcing his wife. This saddens me a great deal, but what can one do?

Unfortunately, the status of the child still remains to be settled.

Although Leonard and Samuel had an active correspondence, only two letters have been discovered among their effects. Both were written during this time period, and are reproduced herein:

April 26, 1943, Dear Pa, Ma, and Sylvia, I'm back in the ole room of mine at Company A, 35th Battalion to await orders for shipment to Benning. I'm told that it may be sometime this week or so . . .

It is a real hot day today . . . Summer is here . . . We go into khaki uniforms on Friday of this week . . .

Pa, I have a little time to myself this evening so I'm sort of going to write about my time in this Man's Army for the past year . . .

Since last April 3rd . . . I have been a combination soldier and gypsy . . . I have been with C Company at Devons, Mass., 38th Battalion, Co. C at Croft, and the following other companies at Croft; Co. C, 27th Bn.; Co. D, 34th Bn.; Co. B, 31st Bn.; Post Headquarters; IRTC; Company A, 35th Battalion; and finally Co. B, 40th Bn. OCPS and also at 2nd CO OCS Regiment at Camp Hood, Texas . . . that's quite a list of residences . . . I have sort of become an expert at un-packing and packing my barracks bags.

I have learned how to march, shoot every infantry weapon, and all that they offer about Army discipline. My stay at the 27th Battalion in the Army Clerk's School taught me a little about Army administration work.

I have marched for miles with full field pack, with combat packs, with machine guns, mortars, rifles, grenades, in the hot sun, in the rain, and through many of these damp and windy days in So. Carolina . . . I have been on night marches, patrols, compass and map problems, both at nite and during the daytime. I have been in tanks, half-trucks, jeeps, peeps, weapon carriers, and large cavalry trailers on troop movements . . . I have eaten the best and the worst type foods the Army offers . . . most of the latter, I can assure you of that.

I have run every type of combat and obstacle course the Army has to offer . . . even the one that has received so much comment in the Army . . . the great combat course at Hood, which is run under live ammunition.

I have qualified as some sort of expert with the bayonet and M1 Rifle [sharpshooter combat infantry badge] . . . I have helped to teach many other fellows how to use these weapons correctly . . . I have had much experience in dirty combat fighting . . . the type of fighting that is contrary to every true principle of American youth and good sportsmanship.

I feel that I have been molded into somewhat of a pattern that classes me as infantry officer material . . . whatever that means. However, I know that I have to stay in this Army and I will try my best to do as much as I can and in the best manner that I can. . . . I admit it has taken me quite a bit of time to earn a commission but my training and the type that I have received just takes that much time and should prove its benefits. . . .

There is much more that I could write about but it just takes so much time and thought . . . and I really am not to [sic] good at the latter.

I haven't heard about your trip to Brooklyn this week-end . . . Tell me all about it . . . Happy Passover. Best regards to all. Your son, Lennie

Shortly thereafter, Leonard wrote the following undated letter:

Sunday Noon: Dear Pa, Ma, and Sylvia, I had a little talk with my Company Commander yesterday afternoon and he promised me that he would arrange a three-day pass for me within the next week . . . Lt. Dobson, my Co. Commander, is quite a man and I think that I can rely upon his word. . . . So, perhaps I may be home by next week-end . . . It's a long drawn-out ride for such a short stay at home . . . but it's worth it.

To Morrow [sic] morning at 9 A.M. I'm scheduled to appear before a board for consideration to attend one of three colleges in the Service Command that I am now located in. It's a long drawn-out matter and I really don't know what to expect . . . it may be well worth trying out for.

You have the right idea about a farm, horse, chickens, dogs, etc. We will have all that when the war is over. I'll make damn sure to that.

Thanks so much for the local newspapers . . . I got them in yesterday's mail call . . . also a few letters from Sylvia. I'll have a lot to tell you when I can get home. Your son, Lennie

These letters are surprising, in large part, by what they omit. Neither Dorothy nor Judy is mentioned. As Samuel indicates, the impending divorce had already been acknowledged in the local newspapers, yet recognition is absent from Leonard's letters. Presumably, these letters survived because of that fact—they contain no reference to Leonard's first wife or child. However, it seems startling to read the letters in the context of the imminent divorce.

Otherwise, the letters provide an intimate glimpse of the relationship between father and son. For instance, Leonard acknowledges his father's fantasy, and commits (i.e., "damn sure") to helping it materialize. Unfortunately, as it turned out, neither Samuel nor Leonard purchased a farm. Interestingly, however, the grandson (Paul Abramson) has harbored a similar fantasy. Though I cannot recall my father's ever expressing this wish, my dreams (as a child) were pervaded with farms. Moreover, when I was in graduate school at the University of Connecticut, I rented a small farm.

I (Paul Abramson) was both pleased and saddened by Leonard's comments about "a farm." First off, I was happy to see that my father and grandfather shared fantasies, and furthermore, it was a fantasy that I valued. However, I was saddened by the fact that it never materialized.

The letters also denote Leonard's pride in his army service. It is clear that he enjoys detailing his many accomplishments. However, Leonard's ambivalence is also evident ("I know that I have to stay in this Army"). Perhaps Leonard's continued failure at Officers Training School belies that ambivalence. Obviously, Leonard was proficient in military regimen (i.e.,"infantry officer material"). However, although he was skilled enough to be considered an officer, he never came through.

It is also interesting to note that Leonard's letters are void of racial slurs. He is not out to kill an enemy, but instead, is trying to be a "good soldier." Not surprisingly, Samuel's diary is also void of racial slurs. Finally, the letters portray an attempt to be clever, humble, and sincere. And for the most part, Leonard succeeds. We wonder, however, what he means by: "It takes so much time and thought . . . and I really am not to [sic] good at the latter"? Was this an acknowledgement of his conscious attempts to deny his family crisis? Or is he merely minimizing his cognitive capabilities?

As far as Samuel is concerned, he seems to have been active during the Jewish holidays. On April 27, Samuel attended the last day of Passover services. He indicates that he led the morning prayers, and "also the *maftir*." *Maftir* means "final portion," and refers to the last three or more verses of holiday Torah reading. Thus, the *maftir* is summoned to the Torah, to recite the blessing prior to the reading of the "final" verses. Afterwards, the *maftir* recites the *haftorah* (meaning the "completion," referring to a portion of the Prophets read after the Torah).

Samuel also indicates that he was given an "English Shas." *Shas* is an abbreviation for *Shishah Sedarim*, meaning the "Six Orders." The "Six Orders" refers to the *Mishna*, which is the earliest written code of Jewish law. The *Mishna* is organized into six sections, called books or "orders." However, at a later date, the *Mishna* was expanded, and then called the Talmud. Moreover, there are two different Talmuds, both of which are written in Hebrew and

Aramaic. The Talmud developed in Israel is called the *Talmud Yerushalmi* (Jerusalem Talmud), whereas the Talmud developed in Babylonia is called the *Talmud Bavli* (the Babylonian Talmud). Samuel is referring to the Babylonian Talmud.

Finally, it is apparent that Samuel records precise details of his son's movements, letters, army serial numbers, and so forth. Why is this information meaningful? What purpose did it serve? Perhaps, Samuel feared for his son's life, and so, all information was worthy of record. Furthermore, the compulsive detailing of dates and numbers could be an unconscious strategy for avoiding disturbing thoughts about his son's mortality.

* * *

It's June 8, 1943. Business is good. This week I took in $569.30. Also, I still have plenty of stock. Unfortunately, however, many wholesalers want to be paid immediately for each bill. But thank God, I have a nice business, and pay my bills on time.

This month I took in $2,205.24, thank God.

We steadily receive letters from Leonard, thank God. And one must hope for the best. Amen, Amen.

It's July 7, 1943. Business is very good. For the week of July 4, I took in $585. Unfortunately, I haven't enough beer. Schaffer brewery stopped delivery, and all that we receive is Connecticut beer. God will help.

Starting on May 29, 1943, my wife Esther has been saving her wages of $10 a week. With God's help, she'll accumulate a few dollars.

On June 21, 1943, I sent for my liquor license. It cost $277.50. The money was drawn totally from my savings. Thank God for everything.

We receive frequent letters from Leonard. Leonard's number in the Army is 11065904.

It's July 26, 1943. Today I sent Leonard $25. He is coming home for 10 days.

It's still hard to get beer, but one goes on. Fortunately, I have plenty of cheap beer—so business is good.

I gave Sylvia a present of $100. Thank God I already have $1,000 in war bonds, and will continue to save. With God's help, all will be good. Blessed be the Lord.

It's August 4, 1943. Leonard came home and had a good time. Also, there was a hearing about his divorce. May he go in good health and come back in good health.

Business is good, but it's still hard to obtain stock. Beer is very difficult to procure, but one hopes that this will change for the better.

During this month of July, I took in $2,669.27. Praise God. However, Leonard's furlough cost me $50.

My wife Esther received $52 for the empty return bottles of Schaffer Beer. She has already $175 in her savings.

It's August 5, 1943. My sister Rachel celebrated her 25th wedding anniversary. Jennie (one of my other sisters) made dinner, and Rachel received fine gifts from the entire family. Leonard was also present, and the following morning he returned to camp. May he travel in good health.

There was a hearing for Leonard's divorce in Bridgeport, Connecticut. The lawyers consulted with each other and came to an agreement. It was decided that we could see Leonard's child every week, and that she'll be brought to our home.

It's August 11, 1943. I received a letter from Leonard that he's back in camp, praise God.

Sunday, he spoke to us over the telephone. Thank God for all. He told us that his wife had sent him a notice of filing for divorce from the Florida Court. In due time, they'll be divorced. I'm not pleased about this, but what can I do? If they can't live together, it's better this way.

I go to services every day, and I hope to God that I will not miss to layn tefillin. Also, every day I praise the Lord for the good he grants us. Amen, Amen.

Bought another government bond. This amounts to $1,200.

It's August 16, 1943. We received a letter from Leonard, stating that he is being sent to Florida, to Blandings Air Force Base. May he be well.

Business is still good. The week of August 16 to August 21 I took in $627.15. This is the best week we've ever had. Praise the Lord.

It's August 19, 1943. We received a letter from Leonard, stating that he arrived at Blandings Air Force Base. May the Lord keep him well. He is now in a Provisional Regiment.

Business is good, but beer is hard to get. Liquor is also difficult to obtain, but nevertheless, one can still get stock. May it not be any worse.

It's August 26, 1943. We receive frequent letters from Leonard. He states that he is satisfied to be in Florida. Also, he became a swimming instructor, with God's help.

The battles appear to be going well, with God's help. It may not be long before the end will come.

Business is good. Earned $640 for the week of August 16-21.

Bought another $100 bond. That makes $1,300 in war bonds, thank God.

Sylvia is leaving for a week's vacation. She worked in Bridgeport, and everything is going well.

It's September 6, 1943. My daughter, may she live, received a telephone call from her friend Raminsky, stating that he's coming to New York. He's now in the service. I hope, with God's help, that they'll marry.

Leonard writes often. May he return to us well.

Business is good, but it's still hard to obtain stock. However, I took in $700 this week, which is very good.

The house where we live was sold, but this time we won't have to drag around to find another one. Now, we hope, with God's help, to be able to buy a home of our own. Amen, Amen.

On May 20, 1943, Leonard Abramson filed for divorce (in Superior Court, Fairfield County, Connecticut). He claimed that Dorothy was guilty of "intolerable cruelty" and "fraudulent misrepresentation concerning matters material to the marriage contract." Moreover, Leonard requested custody of Judith Ellen Abramson.

It is difficult to interpret the meaning of Leonard's accusations. For example, in the absence of no-fault divorce, couples were required to stipulate an acceptable cause for separation. "Cruelty" was convenient, and legally admissible. Thus, the validity of these statements is unclear. Were they realistic, or merely expedient? Furthermore, did Leonard really want custody of Judy? Or did custody represent leverage, to be compromised away, if Dorothy conceded to the divorce? Finally, if custody were granted, where would Judy live? At Camp Croft? Highly unlikely. Instead, she would presumably live with Samuel and Esther. Consequently, since Samuel would profit from custody, we question whether it was Samuel who initiated the proceedings. Perhaps, this was payback to Fannie, the woman he would "never forgive."

On June 5, 1943, Leonard initiated another motion for temporary custody of Judy. Leonard claimed that Dorothy "failed and refused to communicate with him in any manner concerning (Judy's) health, maintenance and welfare . . . and refused to permit (Judy) the right to visit (him or his parents)." Furthermore, Leonard claimed that Dorothy "is not a proper person to have custody of (Judy)," and that for Judy's welfare, Dorothy "should be deprived of her custody pending the final adjudication of this case." Obviously, this is not a congenial divorce. Leonard's accusations are serious and inflammatory. Moreover, his legal actions (and perhaps Dorothy's as well [filed in Florida]) seem punitive and are refractory to a cordial custody settlement.

On August 4, 1943, a compromise was reached. Dorothy was given custody of Judy, but Samuel and Esther were given weekly visitation rights (Sundays, between 3 and 7 P.M.). However, since Leonard is not mentioned in the custody settlement, this is perhaps further evidence that the battle was initiated for Samuel's benefit. Presumably, Dorothy had already assured Leonard that he could visit his daughter. If so, why was Samuel excluded? On the other hand, perhaps Leonard was sufficiently bitter to want to cease all contact with his wife and daughter.

Although temporary custody was resolved, the divorce was still pending. Furthermore, on March 9, 1944, Leonard amended his original complaint to include: "Between May 20, 1943, and March 1, 1944, (Dorothy) committed adultery with a corespondent by the name of Jernigan, of Hollywood, Florida." Was this accusation true? Did it counter a similar complaint by Dorothy? Or was it designed merely to facilitate the divorce—and minimize alimony payments?

On June 24, 1944, Dorothy initiated a motion to revoke or dismiss the custody arrangement. However, the court records indicate that no further actions were taken. Neither the divorce nor the child custody was resolved in Connecticut. Instead, both disputes were settled in Florida. Presumably, since Leonard and Dorothy were now living in Florida, the messy proceedings were conveniently handled outside of Connecticut.

Although Samuel undoubtedly had a hand in this dispute, his contribution is not reflected in the diary. Instead, Samuel frets about trivial details, such as the scarcity of beer. Furthermore, despite substantial income (now more than $20,000 a year), Samuel still seems consumed with obsessive worries.

Samuel's increased anxiety is also evident in his statement "(I go) to services every day, and I hope to God that I will not miss to *layn Tefillin*". Not surprisingly, Samuel's renewed interest in daily ritual corresponds to his heightened fears of death—perhaps his own, and possibly his son's. *Tefillin,* by the way, are small leather boxes that contain four scriptural passages (Ex. 13: 1-10; 11-16; Deut. 6: 4-9; and 11: 13-21). Within these passages are the following three statements: "these words," "A sign upon thy hand and a frontlet between thine eyes," and "thou shalt bind them," which are interpreted in the following manner: The *tefillin* ("these words") are strapped ("thou shalt bind them") to the arm and forehead ("a sign upon thy hand and a frontlet between thine eyes"). Furthermore, *layn* (which in Yiddish means "placing") *tefillin* is intended to induce a feeling of spiritual reverence, and as such has a very significant place in Jewish tradition.

Last, despite prosperity, Samuel continues to quibble over money. Making more than $600 a week, he notes the burden of paying $50 for Leonard's furlough, and the joy of paying his wife a "salary" of $10 a week. Contrary to his benedictions ("Thank God for all"), he often appears reticent to share the wealth.

*   *   *

It's September 8, 1943. My wife Esther deposited $100 in her savings, bringing the total to $600. Thank God.

It's September 25, 1943. Thank God I was able to deposit $327 in our savings account, bringing the total to about $1,000.

We are now looking for a house, but it's hard to find one in the proper location. However, we hope we'll find something.

We receive letters from Leonard. He's about to have a hearing in Miami about his separation from his wife.

It's October 2, 1943. We continue to receive frequent letters from Leonard.

Today, we prayed in the new Jewish Center. The service was very beautiful.

On the 2nd day of Rosh Hashana, Mr. Raminsky visited from camp. Sylvia was very pleased. We hope they'll marry. He's a very fine young man. God should only help. Amen, Amen.

It's October 13, 1943. Leonard wrote that he spent the holidays very pleasantly in camp. God should only help, that next year Leonard will be with us.

As I stated before, Abe Slavitt won the McCarthy case. It's now believed that Leonard will make $800 from this lawsuit.

Business is good, but, as usual, it's still difficult to get stock.

After Yom Kippur evening, I opened the store. I took in $150 in 4 hours. Bless God, that it should not be any worse.

It's October 26, 1943. Leonard was in Miami Beach at a hearing for his divorce. It pains me greatly that he is parting from his wife after such a short time. And what will become of his child? I don't know.

Business is good. I could sell $1,000 worth of liquor a week if I could only get the stock.

One hopes that the war will soon be over. Then all will be good. Praise God.

The week of October 18-23 I took in $726.

It's October 29, 1943. Thank God, I bought a house. It's at 5 Cedar Street, and I purchased it from Michael Steinberg. The price was $7,000, with a mortgage of $5,000. I hope to God I'll be able to pay it off. Let us only be well.

We wrote Leonard—may he be well—that he'll have a home to come back to.

This is how I had money to purchase the house. My wife had $1,100 in her name, and I borrowed $900 from Sylvia. (However, as collateral for Sylvia's money, I gave her my $1,500 in war bonds.) Thus, I had $2,000 in cash.

It's my hope, praise God, that I can repay Sylvia in 6 months, and then use the $1,500 war bonds for the mortgage.

In 1943 Samuel bought a house. It was a family investment. Esther and Sylvia financed the down payment; Samuel provided the collateral.

Despite his prosperity, Samuel has no savings account (except for war bonds). His wife and daughter, on the other hand, had adequate resources. Perhaps Samuel relinquished control over family savings. For instance, in his own estimation, he has been an impulsive investor. Thus, perhaps to minimize future culpability, he now defers to his wife and daughter. Therefore, even though he contributes to a savings account, the account belongs to Esther.

Once again, Samuel enjoyed the holidays, referring to *Rosh Hashana* (the Jewish New Year) and *Yom Kippur* (The Day of Atonement, 10 days after *Rosh Hashana*). On *Yom Kippur*, Jews fast (from food and drink) for 24 hours—and pray throughout the day. Moreover, the time encompassed by the two holidays is devoted to introspection and meditation. Jews reflect upon the past year, and repent feelings, behaviors, and thoughts that compromise intimacy with God.

Rosh Hashana, as explained earlier, is the day that God "records names" in the "Book of Life." Furthermore, on *Yom Kippur*, the book is figuratively "sealed." Therefore, both holidays generate concern and prayer—to be among those sealed in the book of life. Moreover, as inspiration (and as a focus of meditation), the prayers include an often repeated statement: "Prayer, repentance and charity remove the harshness of God's decree."

In 1943 *Yom Kippur* coincided with the Sabbath. The Sabbath (*Shabbas*) covers a 24-hour period, from Friday sundown to Saturday sundown. Furthermore, Orthodox Jews never work on the Sabbath—or on *Yom Kippur,* for that matter, which is the "holiest" day of the year. However, Samuel indicates that as soon as *Yom Kippur* was over (Saturday sundown), he opened his liquor store. During the last 4 hours of Saturday evening (presumably 7 to 11 P.M.), he "took in $150." Unabashedly, Samuel states, "bless God, that it should not be any worse."

Obviously, despite his piety—and prosperity—Samuel considers business to be business, even in the waning hours of the holiest day of the year.

Finally, Samuel is very upset about Leonard's divorce. "It pains me greatly that Leonard is parting from his wife." Unfortunately, the extent of *Leonard's* "pain" is never mentioned. Was Leonard upset? And if so, why? Obviously, divorces are more impacting on the separating spouses and children. However, since this is *Samuel's* diary, perhaps only *his* feelings are stated.

*   *   *

It's November 4, 1943. We continue to receive letters from Leonard. He's very satisfied that we bought the house. May God help, that Leonard will return to us in good health.

It's November 8, 1943. Sunday was the official opening of the new Jewish Center on West Avenue. It attracted a very big crowd, and everything went very well. The Jewish Center is a very fine building. We hope that shortly they will start to build a temple for the Conservative Congregation. Amen, Amen.

It's November 16, 1943. Business is going very well. However, now one can't get whiskey, only dribs and drabs. Yet even so, last week was the best week in the history of our store. We took in $870.91. Thank God for everything.

On Monday, November 15, 1943, my daughter and my sister (Mrs. Slavitt) took title to our home at 5 Cedar Street.

We put down $2,000 and took a $5,000 mortgage, with a $54 monthly payment. This is a 15-year mortgage, and $40 of the monthly payment is for the principal. Thank God for this.

It's November 30, 1943. Mazel tov, Mazel tov. We moved into our new house. Let this be the last move we ever have to make.

Fortunately, the move went very smoothly. We paid Gardella $27 for moving us, plus $15 to clean out our cellar. Painting the house cost $167.

We often receive letters from Leonard. And we hope the war will soon be over.

This week was very good. We took in $770, and we even received some whiskey.

It's December 6, 1943. We are furnishing our new home—and thank God, my daughter Sylvia has helped considerably. The rooms are nice and big, and we are very satisfied.

Little by little, we are receiving whiskey, but it's very difficult to obtain. Fortunately, the store is full of customers. Rum and gin are the best sellers, and we're well-stocked with this for Christmas.

We've settled into our own home, and it feels very warm.

We receive frequent letters from Leonard. He sent us hickory nuts and peanuts from Florida.

It's December 24, 1943. Business is very good. However, liquor is scarce, but gin and rum sell well. Thus, I was able to deposit $300 in my savings account, bringing the total to $500. Now, with God's help, I need only $400 to repay Sylvia.

During the past 4 days, we took in $600.

It's December 29, 1943. Thank God, I was able to repay Sylvia $500. I will shortly return the remaining $400 that was borrowed from her on November 12, 1943. I never would have believed that I could repay her so soon, but God helped, praised be He.

The week of Christmas we took in $1,087.75. This is the best business week we've ever had. Praise God.

It's January 1, 1944. Business was good this week. Also, the month of December netted $3,377.33.

I repaid Sylvia another $100, bringing the total of my repayment to $600. With God's help, I'll return the remaining $300 to her.

It's January 4, 1944. Praise God, I returned another $100 to Sylvia, now bringing the total of my repayment to $700. I will repay her the remaining $200.

A room is being papered, and in due time, all will be done. The gas bill was $28 a month, and it was very warm in our home.

It's January 12, 1944. Business was weaker. One gets only small amounts of liquor.

I was at home for a day—had a cold. The doctor came twice.

We receive frequent letters from Leonard. Everything is fine, thank God.

The house is good and warm.

It's January 25, 1944. On October 29, 1943, I borrowed $900 from Sylvia. And with God's help, I returned it quickly.

Business isn't bad.

We receive frequent letters from Leonard. One must hope that the war will soon be over. Amen, Amen.

Bought a war bond. That now makes $1,700 in government bonds.

Again, I must state that in 6 weeks' time, I was able to return Sylvia's money, thank God.

Within a very short time, Samuel repaid his daughter. The transactions are carefully reported, and his pride duly noted. Yet, what was the rush? And why is this achievement so special?

Sylvia was not without compensation—she had collateral, and shared title to the house. Perhaps Samuel felt guilty (or humiliated) about borrowing money from his daughter—and no "guarantees" were sufficient to eradicate his remorse. Thus, to expiate his guilt (or humiliation), he needed to quickly resolve this debt.

Samuel is also very pleased with the construction of the new Jewish Center. Presumably, the "official opening" was symbolized by placing a *mezuzah* on the main entrance. Originally, *mezuzah* meant "doorpost." However, today, *mezuzah* refers to the small piece of parchment, containing two passages from Deuteronomy (6:9 and 11:20, "And you shall write these words" of God "on the doorposts of your home and on your gate"). This parchment is enclosed in a case, which is attached, slanting inward, to the upper third of the doorpost within every room that Jews live. As Samuel indicates, the Jewish Center was used for a variety of religious and community services. However, as Samuel notes, the center was not a temple, and as such, he prays for the construction of a synagogue.

Finally, Samuel's business continues to prosper (despite his constant obsessions about survival). Although it is unclear whether it is net or gross, his monthly income suggests that he is making more than $30,000 per year.

Incidentally, Samuel's prayer that his "new home . . . be the last home we ever have to make" came partially true. Samuel (but not Esther) lived out his life at 5 Cedar Street, South Norwalk, Connecticut.

*   *   *

It's March 6, 1944. Business is good. We do about $700 a week. We even got some whiskey—Especa gave me nine cases in 2 weeks' time.

Sylvia was in Johnstown, Pa.

The house has been nice and warm for the past 3 months. I paid $108 for gas.

I now have $1,900 in government bonds, and $500 in a savings account—to be used for the mortgage. Also, Raskin did my income tax.

We often receive letters from Leonard. He's preparing to leave for Europe. May God bring him home safely. Also, his divorce is not yet complete.

It's March 7, 1944. Joseph Zashem died—he had gone through a life of hardship. The funeral was held at Ganung's Funeral Parlor. Rabbi Tumin delivered the eulogy. It was a large and impressive funeral.

It's March 13, 1944. Business was good, thank God. We took in about $700 a week. Also, Mr. Raskin created a new accounting system, and charged me $50. I gave him some money in cash, and the remainder I'll owe him.

We did $35,000 in business last year, thank God.

It's March 23, 1944. Leonard is finally getting a divorce. It's been only 2 years, but his marriage was a failure. What can one do? That's life. What one wants isn't always possible.

Now that Leonard is getting a divorce, he and Dorothy have agreed that the child will be raised as a Jewess. It was also agreed that Leonard would continue to have some authority over the child.

I suffer a great deal because of this situation, but I can't do anything to help it. That's life. Now, we must wait and see. Who knows what will happen in the future?

Business is good. Taxes are going up again, and now I have to take inventory every month. Fortunately, I've gotten used to this.

It's March 27, 1944. We have paid $500 toward the mortgage. With God's help, it won't be long before we pay off the entire balance.

On November 15, 1943, we took title to our house, thank God. And though it's hard to believe, in only 4 months' time we've paid $500 toward the mortgage, thank God. The payments grow less with every passing month.

It's March 30, 1944. We receive frequent letters from Leonard. He sent us a box of oranges, which is the second package he's sent. Praise God that he's still in the U.S.A.

The Slavitts and the Leventhals are coming over for Pesach seder. It'll be in our new house. May we be well—and able to overcome life's hardships—Praised be God. Amen, Amen.

It's April 7, 1944. Our entire family came over for Pesach seder, and it was a very fine occasion. Let us hope that we all live to celebrate this again next year. Also, may Leonard be with us, and Sylvia be married. Amen, Amen.

It's April 24, 1944. Leonard called us on the telephone. He finally received his divorce. It still upsets me, but what can one do? That's that. Let God help for the better.

Leonard's furlough was cancelled. The battles are still going strong. Only God knows when this all will end.

For the month of April, I took in $2,647.94 in cash from the store. And for the month of March, I took in $2,831.30.

It's May 29, 1944. We get frequent letters from Leonard. And, thank God, he's still in the U.S. Recently, he was made sergeant. May God help him to return to us unharmed.

Business is the same. You can't get beer, but our income is stable.

It's June 6, 1944. Finally, we hear the news we've been waiting for—the invasion has begun—at 12 midnight. It's hoped that this will bring a swift end to the war.

Our son, thank God, is still in America.

I wish that God could bring all the soldiers back home unharmed.

Business fell a little. Hopefully, with God's help, it'll get better, Amen, Amen.

General Eisenhower ordered the invasion into France at 3 A.M. this morning. Dear God—help us. Amen.

It's July 12, 1944. We went to Brooklyn to celebrate a bar mitzvah—and enjoyed it very much.

God should help, that Leonard will come back to us in good health.

Business has fallen off quite a bit. There isn't enough beer and liquor. However, it'll turn around. It's just a bad time.

Leonard writes frequent letters, and he calls us on the telephone. May he come back to us in good health. Amen, Amen.

Samuel notes that Leonard is "preparing to leave for Europe." This phrase is rather odd, seeming more appropriate for a holiday, or grand tour, than leaving for war. Obviously, Leonard is leaving for battle, as an infantry sergeant, which is certainly a precarious position.

However, from Samuel's commentary, it appears that his inner turmoil is more related to Leonard's divorce. Perhaps the divorce (which is the termination of a relationship) symbolizes Samuel's fears for Leonard's life. The divorce itself, by the way, is treated as an "act of God." Fated, and as such, "what can one do?" However, the record suggests that Leonard and Dorothy were not innocent bystanders. It appears that they were neglectful about contraception, and in turn, embarked upon an ill-advised marriage. Thus, both Leonard and Dorothy share some responsibility for their fate.

Samuel's heartfelt prayers are also evident. Moreover, his prayers are extended to all soldiers, regardless of nationality

("I wish that God could bring all the soldiers back home unharmed".)

Besides praying for Leonard's safe return, Samuel also prays for the marriage of his daughter. This is a constant preoccupation. In 1944, Sylvia is 31 years old.

Why isn't Sylvia married? Has she not found an acceptable suitor? Or is she tied to her parents? Incapable of separating? Feeling guilty and obliged? Interestingly enough, Sylvia's parents have profited from her unmarried status. For instance, she helped purchase, decorate, and maintain the home. In fact, she shares title to the home, which undoubtedly keeps her connected. Finally, she has provided continuous companionship to her anxious and insecure parents. However, these circumstances may soon change. Her father is now solvent, and the home is secure. Thus, perhaps Sylvia will *now* be amenable to marriage.

Finally, as Samuel duly notes, his income continues to grow. At $35,000 per year, he is obviously successful. Yet, when he has to compensate his accountant $50, he is annoyed—and defers payment.

One last comment. Samuel indicates that Leonard and Dorothy agreed that Judy would be raised as a Jew. Since both parents were Jewish, why was this mentioned? Was Samuel concerned about Dorothy's religious commitment? Presumably so.

It is interesting to note that Dorothy ultimately remarried. Her new husband was not Jewish, and evidently, Judy was raised in a non-Jewish household. Thus, to what extent did Samuel anticipate this outcome?

*   *   *

It's July 17, 1944. It was the happiest day of my life. My first grandchild was brought to our home. This is the first time, since Leonard's divorce, that we've seen the child.

She is very beautiful—and bright. And we thank God for the court ruling—that Dorothy must bring us the child every week. We took pictures of the child and sent them to Leonard.

It still hurts us that they've broken up, but what can we do? Anything can happen in life. Fortunately, Dorothy brought us the child. She will be 2 years old on July 31. Praise God for all.

It's July 3, 1944. The child comes every Sunday for several hours. She'll soon be 2 years old. May she continue to live, and always be well—and have a long life.

I bought her a silver spoon and fork. And I hope that we may live to celebrate all her birthdays with her.

Leonard is coming home for a 15-day furlough. Only God knows what will happen afterwards.

I save 25 cents a day for Judy, toward her college education. Bless God. That is my hope and wish.

It's August 8, 1944. Dorothy brought Judy to our home, so that Leonard could speak with his child. Judy is so clever. It makes me angry that they parted. For the child's sake, they should have remained together. Well, Leonard is old enough to know what to do. In the meantime, he's enjoying himself. I pray that God watch over him and bring him home unharmed.

It's August 19, 1944. Leonard left today for Camp Mead, Maryland. May God bring him back to us well. He enjoyed himself here very much. He saw Judy, who becomes prettier and cleverer with every passing day. May God raise her up well. Amen, Amen.

Dorothy returned the diamond ring that I gave to her. I don't understand why she did this. The diamond was originally mine. I'd had it about 35 years. Now, I don't know what my wife will do with the ring.

The baby comes to us every Sunday—what a wonderful child.

It's August 26, 1944. We received a telephone call from Leonard. He's leaving Camp Mead, Maryland. May God bring him home unharmed.

It's August 28, 1944. Leonard sent a telegram stating that he's now at Reynolds Air Force Base in Pennsylvania. He doesn't know how long this will last.

Judy comes to visit us every Sunday—she is very sweet and dear.

It's August 28, 1944. Thank God—we received a telegram from Leonard. He's going to military school. Thank God that he's still in the U.S.A.

Leonard writes us frequently.

It's September 9, 1944. We seem to be winning the war. The fighting is now in Germany itself, and with God's help it'll be over soon.

Leonard is still at Camp Reynolds, Pennsylvania. We hear from him often, and he writes that he's having a good time.

Business isn't bad. I don't have enough beer, but we get plenty of whiskey. And in time, this situation may change. Let us be well.

I have now bought three government bonds ($250) for Judy. May God raise her up well. I'm saving this for her college education, and I've stipulated that this money can only be used for that purpose.

It's September 14, 1944. Leonard is still in Camp Reynolds. However, he'll be in Pittsburgh for the holidays. May God see that he comes back to us unharmed.

Business isn't bad. During the past 8 months, I took in about $22,000. Now, I have enough stock—and I hope, with God's help, to save a few dollars.

It's September 21, 1944. During the holidays, I prayed in the Jewish Center. Also, I led the morning and late afternoon prayers.

I spoke to Leonard prior to Yom Kippur. He is still in Camp Reynolds. Only God knows what will come.

The war is going very well. The Allies crossed the Rhine and are deep in Germany—and we hope the war will end quickly. Amen.

Business is very good—I took in $687 last week. But if I had more beer, I'd do much better. However, thank God for everything.

Samuel is approximately 58 years old. He's been alive for nearly six decades—including 18 years in a Russian village; escaping to America; bringing his family to the United States; marriage; two children; making money—losing it—and finally, making it again; his son marrying, having a child—and then divorcing; and so on. Certainly, it had been a full life. However, on July 17, 1944, something extraordinary happened. According to Samuel, "it was the happiest day of my life."

What made this day the happiest in 58 years? What incredible event achieved this designation? As Samuel attested, it was the day that "my first grandchild was brought to our home." Obviously, Samuel is *shepping naches* (deriving proud enjoyment) from his lovely granddaughter. Furthermore, he expresses intense affection, and genuine pleasure, with Judy's presence. Finally, these feelings are described in a purely loving and uncritical manner. Thus, the intensity of the moment prompted Samuel to declare this day as the "happiest" in his life.

Although Samuel's pleasure is understandable, his designation of the "happiest day of his life" seems surprising. For instance, his "happiest day" is not associated with either his parents, brothers and sisters, children, or wife. Instead, the "happiest" moment is associated with a granddaughter, from a divorced marriage, who disappears shortly after his son remarries. Perhaps, this is Samuel's way of indirectly characterizing his life and family. For example, his diary is filled with pain and disappointment. Conceivably, Samuel was unable to disentangle the pain and disappointment from his feelings about his family. Therefore, he can appreciate his granddaughter—unabashedly and without ambivalence—now that he is prosperous and marginally secure. Certainly, this is not unusual. Many grandparents dote over their grandchildren, who facilitate the illusion of idyllic youth. Moreover, grandchildren provide affection, without excessive responsibility. Thus, when Samuel states that Leonard and Dorothy should have stayed together for "the sake of the child,"—perhaps he also means for the "sake of Samuel." Obviously the divorce, and visitation arrangement (Dorothy has moved hack to Connecticut, and she brings Judy on Sunday afternoons) are not conducive to a long-term relationship between grandfather and granddaughter. Furthermore, Dorothy severed all remaining ties with Samuel ("[she] returned the diamond ring that I gave to her"). Yet, still denying that prospect, Samuel is saving for "Judy's college education."

Besides his affection for Judy, Samuel continues to express attachment and appreciation for his son and daughter.

Perhaps age and prosperity are bringing Samuel's emotions to the foreground. Interestingly enough, remarks about business now account for only 15% of his commentary, in comparison to the comments about his son and daughter, which have increased to 70% of his commentary.

Finally, Samuel indicates that Leonard is "enjoying himself." Is this true? Or is Samuel minimizing Leonard's turmoil? Certainly, at first glance, Leonard's life is anything but idyllic. He was just divorced and lost custody of his child; he has failed Officers Training School at least once; and he is in the infantry (and about to be shipped overseas) during World War II. Is this a time of "enjoyment"? Or is Leonard "lying" to Samuel—and Samuel "believing" it?

On the other hand, Leonard may have been enjoying himself, feeling, "I'm 'free'—and damn it, I'm going to have some fun!"

*   *   *

It's September 30, 1944. Leonard came home for 10 days. He was on leave from Camp Mead, Maryland. He looked good, and said he felt good. Now, he's being sent to California. God should bring him home safe.

I feel like "Father" Abraham, because my good, devoted, and only son has been taken away from me. But what can a person do? It must've been decreed in Heaven. God should return him to us unharmed and healthy. Amen, Amen.

Judy comes to our house every Sunday. She is so lovely and clever, and speaks many words. My joy is indescribable when she says "Goodbye, Grandpa."

It's October 11, 1944. My beloved son is preparing to go to California. May God take care of him.

Judy comes to our house every Sunday—and is so clever and pretty. Also, all the struggles seem worth it, when she comes looking for me, and says "Where's Grandpa?" God should raise her up good.

I made a bed, a bench, and a chest of drawers. It came out very nice.

Business is good—though it's still hard to keep fully stocked. But God will help.

It's November 2, 1944. We received a letter from Leonard, from Oakland, California. He saw Uncle Abe's daughter there.

At present, he's working at the Army Post Office. Only God knows what will be.

Business has been good this month. We took in $3,126.56—making this the best month of the whole year. We should only be well, and Leonard should return to us in good health.

It's November 4, 1944. We receive letters from Leonard regularly. He's still in Oakland, California, and working in the Post Office. Also, his mail is censored.

Judy, may she be well, comes to our house every Sunday—and we have a splendid time. Also, we can't describe how clever she is. She understands every word you say. May God raise her up good—and may we live long enough to derive pride and pleasure from her.

I paid in an additional $300 for the mortgage, and now we owe about $3,800. With God's help, I'll try to pay more.

It's November 24, 1944. Thank God, we continue to receive letters from Leonard. He's still working in the Post Office and he visited my uncle in Oakland, California.

Today is Thanksgiving Day. I closed the store for one hour. We had a turkey dinner, and I drank some beer. If only Leonard could've been with us, we would have had a perfect time. Amen. Amen.

Business is good. During the week of Thanksgiving, I took in $800. Unfortunately, however, liquor can only be purchased in small quantities. Thank God for all.

I paid in $500 toward the mortgage on the house. The balance is now $3,300. With God's help, I'll try my best to pay it off.

On November 29, it'll be one year that we've lived in this house. During this time, I've paid in $1,200 toward the mortgage. Not bad.

Samuel indicates that he feels like "'Father' Abraham, because my good, devoted, and only son has been taken away from me." This comment is in reference to the story of Abraham and Isaac, as presented in the *Torah*. The

Torah narrative suggests that Abraham (and his wife Sarah) waited an extraordinary number of years for a son. Finally, when Isaac was born, Abraham was 100 years old, and his wife Sarah had reached 90 years of age. However, God eventually asked Abraham to sacrifice Isaac. God said, "Take now your son, your only son Isaac, whom you love, and go to the land of Moriah; and offer him there for a burnt offering upon one of the mountains which I will tell you of" (Genesis 22:2).

Although deeply shaken, Abraham conceded to God's wish. He brought Isaac to the place of sacrifice and bound him on the altar. However, at the last minute, the angel of God called Abraham—and told him to stop the sacrifice. As an alternative, the angel pointed to a ram that could be offered in Isaac's place.

The story of Abraham, and the binding of Isaac, has become the quintessential example of self-sacrifice in obedience to "God's will." Obviously, this story has considerable relevance to Samuel. His only son Leonard may soon be sacrificed for his country. Furthermore, since the story of Abraham and Isaac is recited on the second day of *Rosh Hashana*, it is not surprising that Samuel expressed his lament 11 days after this holiday.

Personally, I (Paul Abramson) was deeply moved by my grandfather's comment. His yearning for my father was very touching. Moreover, it surprised me—and made me envious. I was surprised because the sentiment was so powerful. And envious because neither my father, nor I, could express an equivalent feeling. Leonard was not a "good and devoted" father, and in turn, I was not a "good and devoted" son. Thus, Samuel's comment filled a void. He expressed a powerful "wish" about a noble father and his "good and devoted" son, which I experienced as fulfilling a childhood fantasy—a "never-ending bond" that God would not permit to fall asunder.

Samuel continues to enjoy his granddaughter—and concedes that she was worth "all the struggles." Perhaps the custody battle reinforced his commitment to Judy, since the battle appears to have been waged in Samuel's behalf. For instance, when Leonard came home, he and Dorothy went out to lunch, suggesting some degree of communication. Thus, as proposed earlier, the acrimonious dispute may have centered upon Samuel's visitation rights, not Leonard's.

Finally, as consolation (and perhaps distraction) for his troubles, Samuel devotes himself to work. Even on Thanksgiving, when he indulges in beer, he closes his store for only one hour. Furthermore, despite being a gifted craftsman, his diary contains only one reference to this hobby. "I made a bed, bench, and chest of drawers" and it "came out very nice." However, this comment underscores the fact that Samuel was a talented woodworker, whose pieces were not limited to functional furniture. In fact, some of his folk art (e.g., a carved box) has been described (by Steve Rogers, a noted Los Angeles sculptor who was a 1988 recipient of a National Endowment of the Arts Fellowship, and whose work is part of the permanent collection of the Los Angeles County Museum of Art) as "very crafted . . . credible . . . quite good . . . serene . . . and quite professional. He certainly wasn't a backwoods whittler."

Thus, perhaps Samuel found expression for an inner voice, which sought solace and simplicity, in carving wood. If true, this voice was not given much recognition. It barely whispers in the diary.

*   *   *

It's December 4, 1944. A week has already passed, and we haven't heard from Leonard. The last letter we received was dated November 25. We are waiting patiently, and God should bring him home well.

Judy comes this Sunday. She is so clever. We can discuss anything together.

It's December 12, 1944. We still haven't heard anything from Leonard. We are anxiously awaiting news—and it's very hard on us. But how will worrying help? This is life.

Business is good, thank God. Last week we took in $825, which is very nice. Also, we hope to have a good Christmas season. And fortunately, we've quite a bit of stock.

During October and November, we took in $3,100 a month. I hope to be able to pay another few dollars toward the mortgage.

It's December 23, 1944. Thank God, we received a letter from Leonard. He's now aboard ship. Only God knows where they're taking him.

Prior to this, we hadn't heard from Leonard for a month. We pray that God will bring him home safe and sound.

Business has been good for the Christmas season. I'm well stocked with merchandise and have plenty of beer. Also, during the week of Christmas itself, I took in $1,183.80—which is the best week ever.

It's December 26, 1944. On Sunday, I was in Newark, for the funeral of Meyer Sluckt. He was 59 years old. It was a very moving experience.

I paid in another $500 toward the mortgage. There is now a balance of $3,200, and with God's help, it won't take too long to pay it off.

Business is good. I think I'll take in about $4,000 this month.

Leonard arrived in New Guinea, and he writes that it's very hot there. He also requested that we send him a package. May God bring him back to us well and in good health.

It's December 28, 1944. I paid $500 toward the mortgage. Thank God, the balance is now $3,227.64. May it not be any worse.

Today, we sent Leonard two packages. May he return to us safe and sound.

It's January l, 1945. During the past year, the business made $33,227. Of course, I could've done better, if there'd been more beer. We hope to God that next year will not be worse.

We continue to receive letters from Leonard. He's still in New Guinea. We hope that the war ends soon, and that he'll return to us in good health.

During this week of Christmas, we took in more than $1,183.80.

It's January 8, 1945. We continue to receive letters from Leonard—and we also send him packages. He writes that it's still very hot in New Guinea.

Our home is well heated. The gas bill for November and December was $48, which isn't bad.

Business is good. Last month I had 65 cases of liquor, and beer was plentiful.

The week after Christmas I sold $750 worth of spirits. May we be well and not do any worse in the future.

The war is still continuing as before. They are warning us of further bombing expeditions. God should make the war end now.

It's January 16, 1945. Sylvia bought herself a fur coat for $600, although it's worth $960. Also, she insured it for $1,000, because of Michael Jack's recommendation. May she wear it in good health, and God send her the husband intended for her.

It's January 18, 1945. Today I went to Bridgeport, and bought two end tables and two lamps, costing $64.80. May we use them in good health.

Warsaw and Cracow were liberated from the Nazis. Now we hope that the war will be over quickly. Amen, Amen.

It's February 7, 1945. We took in $3,170.50 worth of business for the month of January, but paid out $2,964.01.

Esther has saved $10 a week since last Christmas. Now, she has $250. I hope to God she'll buy herself a nice fur coat.

We receive mail from Leonard quite regularly. His daughter, may she live and be well, becomes lovelier and more charming with each passing week. My deepest satisfaction is when she comes to visit us each Sunday.

Germany is about to surrender. We hope that now the war will be over.

It's February 22, 1945. We got a letter from Leonard on February 17. He writes that he's now on an English ship. We hope to God that we only hear good news from him.

It's February 23, 1945. Thank God, we received another letter from Leonard. He's still aboard an English ship. May God protect him.

Business is good. Although we don't have enough liquor, we're still doing very well. Last week we took in $850. If we had more stock, we could've made $1,000 a week. Thank God for everything.

It's February 28, 1945. Esther and Sylvia went to New York to shop. The weather is a little better; however, it was a very cold winter.

Last month we did $3,000 worth of business.

Business is still good, though liquor is hard to get.

We haven't heard from Leonard for the past week.

It's March 6, 1945. We received a letter from Leonard today. He's now in the Philippines, and may God be with him. He was aboard the English ship for 20 days.

It's April 1, 1945. Aunt Chana died on the second day of Pesach, 17 days in Nissan. She was 80 years old. At the end of her life, she was very sick. May her death be an atonement for us all.

Business is good. We take in about $800 a week.

We still receive frequent letters from Leonard. It's hoped that the battles with Germany will soon be over.

This Pesach seder was held in my house—and my mother was with us. May she be well.

Judy is prettier and more clever than ever.

We paid in another $500 toward the mortgage. The balance is now $2,500. Thank God.

Leonard is no longer in the United States. He has gone to war. And for an entire month Samuel has lost track of his son. Is Leonard safe? Is Leonard in battle? Is Leonard alive? Samuel doesn't have a clue. Thus, he "anxiously await(s) news," and finds the uncertainty "very hard." Yet, despite his turmoil, Samuel introduces a very curious thought, "how will worrying help? . . . This is life."

This statement is curious for several reasons. First, Samuel worries all the time. He worries about beer, the mortgage, his daughter's prospects for marriage, money, and so forth. However now, in the face of adversity he becomes philosophical, deferring to fate. While this attitude is not without merit, it seems paradoxical in a man plagued with petty worries.

Eventually, Leonard arrives in New Guinea, and shortly thereafter, the Philippines. Samuel indicates that Leonard writes often. Presumably, these letters contained information about Leonard's life—yet only the weather ("still very hot") is recorded in Samuel's diary. For instance, Leonard sent a picture of himself, from the Philippines, surrounded by tribes people. The caption reads: "Taken at Dupax-Aritao, Cagayan Valley, Philippines. (These people are) Igorots . . . the last of the tribes of Mountain People in the PIs . . . most of them are English-speaking (,) having been taught by an active Order of Belgium Priests. The boy at my left is wearing my fatigue cap . . . I left most of (my) clothing with this family. Lennie." Perhaps neither father nor son wrote about the war.

It is also interesting to reiterate that neither father nor son expressed racial prejudice. In more than 200 pages of diary, which includes World War II, there is neither a single racial slur nor profanity attached to a racial or national group. The Germans are either "Germans" or "Nazis"—not "fucking Germans" or "fucking Krauts." Furthermore, even in Leonard's letters, such as the note above, there are no disparaging comments about racial origin. In fact, Leonard's description of the Igorots displays considerable thought and sensitivity, especially for a sergeant in the Army in 1945.

Back home, Samuel continued his usual pursuits. Now 60 years of age, his is witnessing the death of his peers. First, he mentions that Meyer Sluckt's funeral was "moving." Presumably, it was moving because, in part, it touched close to home. However, where Samuel's Aunt Chana is concerned, he states that her death should "be an atonement for us all."

Historically, atonement was accomplished through sacrifice. Today, in the Jewish religion, atonement means the reconciliation between humans and God, as a consequence of sin that damaged that relationship. Atonement is achieved through repentance, suffering, and/or death—depending on the severity of the transgression. Thus, for atonement to be effective, a person can be purified through prayer, repentance, and charity. Moreover, if the sin is great, suffering is another means of atonement. Finally, death is the ultimate atonement for sins. When close to death, the following formula may be recited: "May death be an atonement for all my sins."

It is interesting to note that Samuel changes this prayer to read "May death be an atonement for us all." While this is a common Yiddish expression, it is not a Jewish concept. For instance, while Jesus is believed to have died to atone for others' sins, the Jewish prophet indicates that "every man shall die for his own sin" (2 Ch 25:4). Nevertheless, perhaps Samuel considered the death of an important family member to be a pardon for the entire family's sins. On the other hand, maybe this is an expression of his own guilt (and hence sin). Earlier in the diary, Samuel states that he "didn't get along with Tante Chana, and lived elsewhere." Perhaps he always resented her (at some level), and her death provoked his guilt. Furthermore, while Meyer Sluckt's funeral moved him, his Aunt Chana elicited atonement.

Finally, despite a very full life, Samuel's "deepest satisfaction" continues to be associated with Judy. He sees her for only 3 hours a week, but she seems to provide the greatest pleasure. Perhaps he enjoys the simple, uncomplicated, and unthreatening nature of their interaction. He gives, she receives. And vice versa.

*   *   *

It's April 12, 1945. President Roosevelt has died, at 64 years of age. It's a great pity that he couldn't see the end of the war. And now that he's dead, the Jewish people have lost their best friend.

It's April 21, 1945. Russia invaded Germany. I hope she'll treat the Germans like they treated her.

The World Conference was held in San Francisco on April 25. We'll see what this conference will do for the Jews.

Business is good, thank God.

We receive frequent letters from Leonard, but it's hard to wait for them to arrive. God help that the war will be over soon.

Judy visits every Sunday. And every week she becomes prettier and more clever. Now, she understands as much as a 5-year-old child. Also, she brings us so much joy.

In August, Judy will be 3 years old, and I'll have a $100 bond for her birthday. May she live a long life.

It's May 1, 1945. The war is about to end. Mussolini was shot by the Italian people. His body, and the body of his girlfriend, were hung by their feet—for display—in the city of Milan.

It's May 8, 1945. Thank God the war in Europe has ended with an unconditional surrender.

We received a letter from Leonard. He's now a staff sergeant. Thank God.

Judy is growing up to be a very lovely child. Thank God.

Business is good. I paid another $100 toward the mortgage.

We received a letter from Leonard. He's in a hospital in the Philippines. He was wounded on April 23. God send him a sure cure.

It's May 10, 1945. We received three letters from Leonard. He's now walking on crutches. I thank God for this. We're waiting impatiently to hear from him.

Also, Leonard has received the Purple Heart. He's going to send the medal to us. Please God, help him come home to us, cured and well.

It's May 11, 1945. We received four letters from Leonard. He writes that he's better.

Also, Dr. Abramson sent me a letter he received from Leonard. Leonard writes that he was wounded in the foot. God should help him.

Leonard was in the 34th Division. I pray to God that we'll hear good news from him.

It's May 14, 1945. We continue to receive letters from Leonard. He mentions that Dr. Skluth went to visit him. He also states that he's getting better and that he's now in a convalescent hospital, where he's received 100 letters, and 10 packages from us. God bring him home healthy.

Business is the same, but now I've plenty of beer.

I bought two additional $100 bonds for Judy.

God should bring my son home, well and healthy.

It's June 1, 1945. Business was good this month. I brought in $3,300. Also, I paid $250 toward the mortgage, with the balance being about $2,000. God should grant us good health, so that we can pay off the mortgage quickly.

We receive many letters from Leonard, stating that he feels better. May God send him back to us well. Amen, Amen.

It's June 5, 1945. We continue to receive letters from Leonard. He writes that his wound is healing. May God send him a cure. Amen, Amen.

Business is good. Last week we brought in $800, but it's still hard to get good liquor. However, I'm sure this will eventually iron itself out. But one must wait.

I bought two government bonds for myself, and one for Judy. Esther and I now have $2,400 in bonds, to be used in our old age.

If I don't make provisions for us, who will? And if I don't do it now, when will it be done?

It's June 20, 1945. We receive frequent letters from Leonard. Although his wound is healing, it's taking time. We hope that he comes home quickly (and we live to see him), because it's hard for us to wait. But one must be patient.

It's now been 3 weeks since we've seen the baby. Her mother is playing politics with us, but she won't get away with it.

Business is good, and I have plenty of beer. Last week, we generated $700 worth of business. And on Friday and Saturday, we took in over $400, thank God.

Now, all we need is to have Leonard come home well. Amen, Amen.

It's June 21, 1945. We received four letters from Leonard. He sent us the bullet that was removed from his foot. Thank God he is recuperating successfully. We hope we can see him soon.

It's July 5, 1945. The 4th of July has now passed, and everything's okay. Business was good, and we had plenty of beer. In fact, in 3 days, we took in $375. Fortunately, we now have a good stock of merchandise. May we just be well.

We receive frequent letters from Leonard and we received his Purple Heart. May God bring him home well.

Judy is once again coming every week. May God protect her with good health.

It's July 17, 1945. We receive frequent letters from Leonard. His wound is healing nicely. May God bring him good health.

On the 31 of July, Judy became 3 years old. We had a party and bought her a beautiful doll. May she have a long life.

Business was very good. For the month of July, we took in $3,100. However, I've a bit too much stock, but with God's help, it'll sell.

It's August 14, 1945. For the last 3 days, we've been waiting for the news, and finally Japan made an unconditional surrender on August 15, at 7 P.M. Thank God, the war is over.

We continue to receive letters from Leonard. He's now out of the hospital, and we hope to see him shortly. Thank God for all.

Business is good. During the last 2 weeks we took in more than $1,700.

Now, we're waiting for Leonard to come home, safe and sound. Amen, Amen.

It's August 29, 1945. We hear from Leonard frequently. As of now, he's back with his company. Only God knows how long he'll remain there. However, we hope that he'll come home shortly.

Sylvia left for Canada on a vacation. May she return in good health.

Business is good, and I get plenty of merchandise. May we all be in good health.

MacArthur has taken over in Japan. And that marks the end of the Japanese Military Command.

It's September 6, 1945. Today, we received a letter from Leonard. He's back in the hospital. We hope he'll be able to come home soon.

Business is good. Last week brought in $875. This is very good.

A new year is coming. May we live and be well. And may God give us a good livelihood.

Judy is growing up beautifully. May God watch over her.

Sylvia was in Canada and had a good time.

It's September 15, 1945. There was a little news clipping in the Central News about Judy Abramson.

We receive frequent letters from Leonard. He writes that he's feeling better and that he has rejoined his company.

Now, it's very hard for us to work, waiting for his return. May God bring him back healthy.

Business is good. May we just have a healthy year.

It's October 1945. Yom Tov has passed, and all went well. My mother was with us for Simchas Torah, and I was the ba'al tefilah at the Jewish Center. We enjoyed ourselves very much.

We receive frequent letters from Leonard. He writes that he hopes to be home shortly, perhaps by Christmas. May God help him.

Judy is growing up to be a very clever child. She speaks very well.

It's October 24, 1945. We went to a wedding in Brooklyn, for my brother-in-law's (Sam) son. We had a very enjoyable time.

We've not heard from Leonard. Perhaps he's on his way home, with God's help.

Business is good. We get plenty of stock now. Last week, we took in more than $800. We are doing very well, thank God. Also, the balance on the mortgage is now $1,623. And with God's help, the mortgage will be paid off shortly. Thank God.

It's November 9, 1945. We got a letter from Leonard. He's in Japan, but may be leaving soon. And with God's help, he may be here by Thanksgiving.

Business is good. We get plenty of beer and liquor. Also, we're taking in about $800 a week, which is very good.

The balance on the house is now $1,400.66.

Judy is so delightful, clever, and lovely. May God give her many years.

It's November 20, 1945. We continue to receive letters from Leonard. He's still in Japan, but we hope he'll come home soon. He writes that he's been shopping in Japanese department stores and that he sent us a package with some Japanese goods.

Leonard's daughter is getting lovelier each day. May she continue to be well.

The balance on the mortgage is now less and less.

We have $2,800 in war bonds.

It's November 27, 1945. We received a letter from Leonard, stating that he's leaving Japan on November 15, 1945. We are waiting impatiently to see him. May God give him health.

Business was very good for this Thanksgiving week. We took in $1,035.90. Thank God for everything.

It's December 6, 1945. On Thursday, in the month of "Teves, Parshas Miketz, my uncle Gedalia passed away. He was 92 years old. May he rest in peace.

We haven't received any more letters from Leonard. We're waiting impatiently to hear from him. It's very difficult for us.

May God help us, so that we can hear from him shortly. Amen, Amen.

It's December 18, 1945. Today we received a telegram from Leonard. He's already in the United States, in Tacoma, Washington. We hope to see him soon. Praise God for bringing him home well. It's been 3 years and 8 months since he enlisted in the Army.

It's December 22, 1945. We received a telegram and spoke with Leonard on the phone. We're waiting to see him.

Business is good.

The weather is cold, and there's a lot of snow.

It's December 26, 1945. We're still waiting to see Leonard.

Business was good last week, especially Christmas. Prior to Christmas, I made $601.25. Including Christmas, my income was $1,135.05. Now, I have sufficient money to pay the bills. Thank God for everything.

It's December 29, 1945. I received a telegram from Leonard today. He'll be arriving at Camp Devons. We are waiting impatiently to see him at last.

It's January 4, 1946. Leonard is now in Camp Devons, receiving medical treatment. And although he calls us every day, it's still very hard for us to wait. However, we hope to see him soon.

Business was very good this month. During December, we took in $4,632, the best month we've ever had, thank God.

It's January 7, 1946. Leonard finally came home. He was on a 3-day furlough. He doesn't look bad, except he looks a bit yellow, no doubt from his fever. But it was a pleasure to see him.

His daughter welcomed him in a very friendly manner.

We all enjoyed ourselves with Leonard.

The house on Bouton Street was sold for $2,700. My sister Jennie is holding the money for our mother.

Business is very good.

Leonard Abramson was wounded in battle on April 23, 1945. He was shot in the right thigh by Japanese gunfire. Immobile and abandoned, he was eventually rescued when the threat of further attack had ceased.

Leonard's military records indicate that as a result of his wound (GSW—right thigh), he spent 5 months in a military hospital, during which time he also suffered from hepatitis for 9 weeks. Finally, in conjunction with his other injuries, Leonard tested positive for malaria on 10 occasions, requiring additional hospitalization for 2 weeks in December, 1945.

Obviously, Leonard's injury and his recuperation were considerably more severe than a "wound in the foot" that "heal(ed) nicely." Thus, why the discrepancy? Was Leonard minimizing the extent of his injury, which left a permanent indentation in his thigh and gave him a military disability? Or did Samuel "hear" only what he wanted to hear: The wound was minor and everything was okay.

Perhaps there is evidence suggesting that both father and son intended to minimize this crisis. For example, as noted previously, Samuel minimized, or distorted, significant events (e.g., Leonard's flunking out of college). Similarly, throughout his life, Leonard Abramson denied the severity of his circumstances. For instance, when dying of cancer, he convinced his family that it was "benign," and that his surgery was successful. Furthermore, when he went back to the hospital for additional surgery, he stressed that it was only a "minor complication." However, the following night he died of a heart attack (at 59 years of age). After his death, his physician indicated that Leonard Abramson had been told, in no uncertain terms, 9 months previously, that the tumor was malignant, and was expected to prove fatal within one year.

Thus it appears that Leonard had the capacity to withhold information on the severity of an illness, which may have some relevance to both his wound in 1945 and his father's impression of that injury. Of course, we also wonder why Samuel ever questions why a "foot injury" would require 5 months' hospitalization.

Perhaps, it was an unwritten rule that Samuel and Esther had suffered enough, and that additional trauma was not allowed. If so, it had a profound impact upon their son. Sick and wounded, in a makeshift military hospital in the Philippines, Leonard writes that everything is "just fine."

Even if Leonard minimized his situation, Samuel was clearly distressed about his son. "May God bring him home healthy" and "may we live to see him." Obviously, Leonard's injury also stirred Samuel's fears about Leonard's mortality.

Yet, despite his worry, Samuel seems surprisingly complacent. In fact, he provided the following information for a local newspaper story:

Monday, May 14, 1945 STAFF SGT. ABRAMSON WOUNDED IN ACTION Staff Sgt. Leonard Abramson, son of Mr. and Mrs. Samuel Abramson of 5 Cedar Street, was wounded in action in Luzon, according to word received by his parents. He is now on the road to recovery and has been awarded the Purple Heart which he has sent to his parents.

This story, by the way, appeared only 3 weeks after Leonard was wounded.

Leonard eventually made it back to the United States. On December 20, 1945, he sent the following telegram to his father:

SAMUEL ABRAMSON=
73 RAILROAD AVE F ONE 8-9689 SOUTH NORWALK CONN= ARRIVED TACOMA YESTERDAY NOW AT FT LEWIS AWAITING TRAIN FOR DEVONS LONG TELEPHONE DELAYS WILL TRY BEST TO CALL IF POSSIBLE IM OK SHOULD BE HOME WITHIN TEN DAYS LOVE=LENNIE.

Samuel was obviously very pleased to receive this telegram, and stated, "Praise God for bringing him home well." Remarkably, this is the only (existing) letter that Leonard signed with "love." Presumably, coming home to America and family—after being wounded in action—was enough to justify "love."

However, when Leonard finally arrived, the reunion is suspiciously understated. Perhaps, once again, Samuel is overwhelmed, creating an emotional inhibition. On the other hand, maybe Samuel was disappointed. Leonard the "real son" was not Leonard the "idealized son" (from Samuel's "fantasy"), who could be loved from afar. Finally, perhaps the intimacy frightened Samuel. Here was Leonard, the long-lost son, wounded by Japanese gunfire and sick in body and spirit, but home at last. Conceivably, the intense homecoming (and Leonard's affection and neediness) may have intimidated Samuel.

Besides worrying about Leonard, Samuel also worried about his retirement, "If I don't make provisions for us, who will?" This comment is derived from a *Mishna* (i.e., "teaching") in the Saying of Our Sages (Ch. 1; 14), which is translated as follows:

> He (referring to Hillel) used to say: If I do not do for myself, who will do it for me? And if I care only for myself, what am I? And if not now, when?

Paradoxically, Samuel used this *Mishna* out of context, since the original saying referred to "spiritual aspirations." In fact, the line "if I care only for myself" is a denigration of personal/material needs. Thus, the intent of the *Mishna* is to facilitate spiritual fulfillment by stressing the importance of self-reliance in spiritual endeavors. In contrast, Samuel contorted the *Mishna* to mean, "Save your own money, because no one else will save it for you."

Samuel also expressed his sorrow over the death of FDR. "It's a great pity, that he couldn't see the end of the war. And now that he's dead, the Jewish people have lost their best friend." Certainly, most Jews supported Roosevelt, and Roosevelt in turn, supported the Jews. However, history has demonstrated that Roosevelt was not always the "best friend" to the Jewish people. For instance, it is clear that Roosevelt knew more about the Nazi death camps than he publicly admitted. In fact, the concentration camps were common knowledge, yet Roosevelt failed to prohibit the deportation of Jews. Finally, Roosevelt never lifted immigration quotas, thereby condemning many Jews to certain death.

In addition to following the progress of the war, Samuel was also concerned with the impact of the nascent United Nations, "We'll see what this Conference will do for the Jews." Presumably, Samuel was referring to Great Britain's limitation on Jewish immigration into Palestine. Perhaps Samuel was hoping that Great Britain would now introduce a resolution to change Palestine from Mandate rule to autonomous rule, in light of the current momentum for a Jewish national homeland.

Finally, Samuel continues to enjoy his granddaughter. Judy appears responsive to both grandfather and father, despite the long absence. However, trouble looms in the offing. Judy doesn't visit for 3 weeks, which "coincidentally" followed the newspaper clipping about Leonard's being wounded. Perhaps Dorothy was awaiting news of Leonard's condition. Conceivably, Dorothy may have concluded that if Leonard dies, Samuel's visitation would correspondingly cease. However, as news of Leonard's survival (and decorations—Purple Heart, Bronze Star, and so on) trickled back to Norwalk, the visitation was reinstated. Last, Samuel kept a small newspaper clipping about Judy:

(September 15th) Envy of all her playmates is three-year-old Judy Abrahamson, sparkling daughter of Dorothy Safir, with her crown of jet curls and big, black eyes to match.

Although this article appeared in only a minor newspaper, it illustrates the small-town nature of Norwalk, Connecticut. Moreover, the article gives further evidence of Leonard's diminished relationship with his daughter. Judy is now "Abrahamson"—not Abramson—a minor but perhaps significant error.

*   *   *

It's January 8, 1946. Leonard left for Camp Devons today. He'll be there a week.

Thank you, God, for everything, that we lived to see our son come home.

We're supposed to see Leonard again shortly.

Business isn't bad. I'm able to pay the December bills and I also hope to make a payment on the mortgage. Thank you, God, for everything.

It's January 19, 1946. Thank you, God, for everything. If one lives long enough, one will achieve good things.

Leonard came home today on a furlough. He looks better and, fortunately, he can stay longer.

Esther bought a fur coat, and it fits her very well. May she wear it in good health. She certainly has earned it. And she used her own money, saving $10 a week in a Christmas Club.

Business, thank God, is very good.

It's January 29, 1946. Leonard is back in Camp Devons, but he can come home on weekends. He looks better, and we hope he'll soon be free of Army service.

I paid another $200 toward the mortgage, and the balance is now $989.24.

It's February 3, 1946. Leonard, may he live and be well, was finally discharged from the Army. Thank God for all.

This week business was good. I took in $900, which is very good. I also paid $200 toward the house. Thank God for everything.

We went to New York for Robert Leventhal's wedding. We had a good time, and a lovely supper was served. However, the greatest pleasure was to have Leonard with us. Now, may I live to celebrate my daughter's wedding.

My wife Esther wore a lovely dress, together with her new fur coat. She looked wonderful.

It's February 11, 1946. On Saturday, I was at the Jewish Center, where I donated 2 quarts of liquor and a gallon of wine. I also prayed and afterwards gave a very nice kaddish.

On Thursday I was also in shul, and donated 2 quarts of liquor and refreshments. Thank God for all. May I be able to continue giving in the future.

Business is good. Last week I took in $800. However, it was hard to obtain liquor. But God will help.

Leonard feels better. Thank God for everything.

I paid $200 toward the mortgage. Now the balance is $589.24. It won't be long before the house is all paid off. Praise the Lord for everything.

It's February 18, 1946. Business is good. Last week we took in $850, and paid in $300 on the house. The balance is now $289.24. Praise God.

Leonard is enjoying himself and he looks much better. I hope to God he will soon be his old self.

We had company from Brooklyn. Aunt Chana and the whole family (17 people in all) were at our house. We had a good time.

It's February 25, 1946. Business is about the same.

Leonard, praise God, feels much better. God will help, and he'll be healed.

I paid $100 toward the house. The balance is now $153. With God's help, I'll quickly pay off the remainder. Praise God.

It's February 26, 1946:

Congratulations, Congratulations. Thank God I've paid off the mortgage, and the house is now free and clear.

This house was purchased October 29, 1943, and in the short period of 2 years and 3 months, I paid it all off. The house cost $7,000, with $500 for the additional expenses of painting and plumbing.

Thou hast loosed my sackcloth, and girded me with gladness. Thank God for everything. Amen and Amen. If I am not for myself, who will be for me, and if not now, when? (signed) Samuel Abramson

Samuel indicates that he "gave a very nice *kaddish.*" *Kaddish* literally means "sanctification." Thus, to "keep the Sabbath holy" (Torah, Ex. 20:8), a prayer (i.e., *Kaddish*) is recited (over a cup of wine, usually in the home), as an act of sanctification.

The primary *Kaddish* is recited on Friday night; however, a second *Kaddish* is recited on Saturday (the Sabbath)

prior to eating the midday meal. Recently, synagogues have also started having *Kaddish* within the temple. The temple *Kaddish* often serves as a social hour for the congregation.

To share the spirit (and cost) of the *Kaddish,* the congregants usually take weekly turns donating food and drink. Wine, liquor, cake, cookies, fish, fruit, and so on are among the donations. Since Samuel donated his wine and liquor on a Thursday, it was presumably for a future Sabbath. Furthermore, it is unlikely that 4 quarts of liquor and a gallon of wine would be consumed at a single *Kaddish.* Thus, his gift was probably used over a period of several weeks.

Samuel also mentions the phrase "thou hast loosed my sackcloth." This is from the second half of the 12th verse in the 30th chapter of Psalms. The second half of Psalm 30 reads:

"And in my prosperity I said, I shall never be moved. Lord, by Thy favor Thou hast made my mountain to stand strong: Thou didst hide Thy face, and I was frightened. I cried to Thee, O Lord; and to the Lord I made supplication. What profit is there in my blood, when I go down the pit? Shall dust praise Thee? Shall it declare Thy truth? Hear, O Lord, and be gracious to me: Lord, be Thou helper. Thou hast turned for me my mourning into dancing: Thou hast loosed my sackcloth, and girded me with gladness; to the end that my glory may sing praise to Thee, and not be silent. O Lord my God, I will give thanks to Thee forever."

Obviously, Samuel does give "thanks to God"—over and over again. Furthermore, Samuel interprets the Psalm in the following manner: "Thou hast loosened my sackcloth of poverty and deprivation, and now, thou hast girded me with the gladness of prosperity and security." However, not surprisingly, Samuel's interpretation is idiosyncratic. The author of the Psalm, King David, intended no such meaning (according to Rabbi Shimshon Rafael Hirsch). Instead, David implied the opposite: That prosperity leads to moral stagnation, and furthermore, that tribulations are not cause for mourning, but rather gladness, since adversity facilitates the fulfillment of God's will.

This distortion of the Psalms is similar to Samuel's mis-representation of the teaching, "If I am not for myself." As discussed earlier, this teaching refers to spiritual self-reli-ance, not a personal pension plan. Thus, perhaps Samuel's distortion of traditional sayings yields insight into his personal perspective. For instance, obviously, as a result of his education in Russia, he was conversant with the Old Testament. Furthermore, Samuel's use of tradi-tional sayings reveals the extent to which he identified with his Jewish heritage, albeit in a somewhat idiosyn-cratic manner. Finally, Samuel uses traditional sayings to express his joy and triumph. Consequently, paying off the mortgage has transcendental meaning to him.

Yet, given Samuel's constant worries, perhaps he might have been happier if he experienced the broader meaning of spiritual enlightenment. Instead, as the diary suggests, it seems that Samuel searched elsewhere. He sought secu-rity and happiness from "shallow" dollars. And in the pro-cess, it appears that Samuel got "lost on the streets of gold."

Besides personal worries, Samuel is also concerned about Leonard's health. Presumably, Leonard was still ex-hibiting the aftereffects of malaria and trauma. However, despite these concerns, Samuel is genuinely pleased to have his son at home: "The greatest pleasure was to have Leonard with us." Finally, Samuel also mentions that "Leonard is enjoying himself." This is an extraordinary comment. It is the first time that Samuel uses the word *enjoy* without an external reference, such as money or prosperity. Obviously, Leonard was just happy to be home, and clearly exhibiting his satisfaction.

*   *   *

It's March 15, 1946. Business was good. However, my in-come tax was $600. Also, the state tax was $34, and $50 went to Raskin for preparing the tax statements.

Leonard feels better, and in the meantime, he stays at home. He needs a good rest. I give him $10 a week for ex-penses. May he be well.

Judy is growing up beautifully. I bought her a bicycle in Bridgeport for $20. She has lots of fun with it. May the Lord grant her good health.

This is Leonard's Veteran's Administration Claim Number, C-8931-010. His Army Serial # is 11065904.

I bought a daybed at a cost of $45. May we use it in good health.

It's April 22, 1946. Pesach was at the Slavitts, and my mother was at the seder. Also, Leonard was finally with us, after 4 years in the Army. It was very joyous. Thank God.

Business is good. The week before Pesach and Easter I took in $1,000. During the second week, I took in $800. We lack beer, but God will help.

My mother was with us the entire week of Pesach. We bought a bed for her. May she enjoy herself, and may she live to celebrate the next year with us.

It's June 10, 1946. Shavuos has already passed. My mother was with us for an entire week.

Business is good, but we don't have enough beer and liquor. However, wine is selling well.

Leonard wasn't feeling well, but thank God, he's now better. Unfortunately, he still has some fever. We hope he'll be well soon.

Leonard is now painting the trim around the house. And we are also laying a new roof. The roof cost $1,274, and Niari did the construction.

Recently, we've had some other trouble with the house. Digging cost $75. Plumbing cost $70, and fixing the chimney cost $15.

I bought Judy a pair of ice skates. She's growing up beautifully. May she be well.

It's June 28, 1946. Leonard painted the trim, and the paint cost $25. May he be well.

Business is good, but beer is hard to get.

Today, I bought a pair of gold earrings for Esther, at a cost of $125. Praise God. May she wear them in good health. She certainly has earned it.

Business is good. We now do about $800 a week. Thank God, we can save a dollar.

We also pray to God that we'll live to see our children happy.

The baby is more adorable day by day. May God take care of her.

It's July 22, 1946. Arthur Niari fixed the roof of the house, and it cost an additional $300. But I paid him on the spot, thank God. Now, the house is in good shape. May God also help us make a good living during this next fall and spring.

Business is good, and we have plenty of stock. Let us just be well.

It's July 29, 1946. Judy, may she live a long life, had another birthday party. This July 31 she'll be 4 years old. May the Almighty take care of her—and give Leonard and Dorothy more common sense on how to behave and how to raise her well. Furthermore, I still feel hurt because of the mistake my son made.

Judy received lovely gifts.

Perhaps, Samuel still feels "hurt" about Leonard's "mistake" because the divorce has compromised Samuel's relationship with Judy. Apparently, these feelings have resurfaced because Leonard is back at home, and Samuel is seeing more of his granddaughter. Coincidentally, the additional exposure has also elicited more generosity from Samuel (e.g. he buys Judy a bike and skates).

Yet, at some level, Samuel must be aware that his relationship with Judy is ill-fated. Dorothy, a single mother in the 1940s, is obviously going to remarry. The same is true for Leonard. Therefore, the most probable outcome is that Judy will become absorbed into her stepfamily, as Leonard also pursues a new life. And while at present there is greater continuity for children of divorced parents, in 1946 it was relatively unheard of.

On the other hand, perhaps Samuel is "living for today." Judy is "his" granddaughter, and he is trying to make the best of the current situation.

Incidentally, Samuel's generosity is not limited to Judy. He bought his wife an expensive gift and he is presently supporting his son. However, an "allowance" of $10 a week, from a man making more than $30,000 per year, is paltry compensation, given that Leonard is working around the house despite his disability. Also, Samuel's appreciation for his wife seems unduly connected with money. In the last section, Samuel described Esther as "lovely." However, this unique flattery was reflecting the fact that Esther was wearing a new dress and fur coat.

Last, it is conceivable that our interpretations are excessively harsh, that is, begrudging Samuel his expenditures. For example, Samuel is now prosperous, and one might argue that he deserves to spend his money. However, in turn, we believe (given our own biases) that his generosity would be better appreciated if he seemed happier and not so obsessed with picayune expenses.

*   *   *

It's October 29, 1946. Summer is over, and business was good. Now, we can get plenty of stock. In fact, we had over 85 full cases of liquor, and we do about $800 worth of business a week.

At present, Leonard is working in the store. What he plans to do in the future, I don't know. However, he's old enough to make up his own mind.

My mother will 80 years old this month. May she be well. She was with us during this entire month of Jewish holidays.

It's November 10, 1946. My sister Jennie had a birthday party for our mother, who just turned 80 years old. It was a wonderful party, with all the trimmings, including a turkey dinner and birthday cake. Mother felt good, and her mind was clear. May the Lord grant her more years.

During the month of Cheshvan, I turned 62 years old. May God grant me health. Also, I'm now on diet and losing weight. Prior to the diet, I weighed 217 pounds. Now I weigh 190 pounds. Dr. Berk is my doctor.

Business, thank God, is good.

It's November 28, 1946. Today we had a lovely Thanksgiving dinner. Fortunately, Judy also joined us. In fact, we all had a good time, and I hope that we can celebrate this together again next year. Finally, may God provide a good husband for my daughter.

Business is good, thank God.

It's December 26, 1946. Christmas is now over. Business was good, about the same as last year. In fact, the day before Christmas, we took in $600, with the total business for the month amounting to over $4,000. Thank God for everything. Also, we hope that these times will remain good.

Leonard began working in a real estate office. He says that he plans to go to school.

Judy is growing up to be a fine young child. May God watch over her. And thank God for everything.

It's January 11, 1947. Thank God for everything. It was a good year, and the business took in over $45,000. In fact, on the two days before New Year's, I took in $535 each. It was very nice.

May we live and be well. And thank God for all.

It's January 11, 1947. Chana Ziselman, my wife's sister, died today, Parshas Shmos. She was 63 years old and had been sick a long time.

It's January 11, 1947. I've been going to the Jewish Center for 6 weeks straight.

It's March 5, 1947. Today I was at the Jewish Center, where I read the megillah.

Thank God for everything—that I'm still here and that I was able to survive my illness.

It's March 28, 1947. Rabbi Tumin retired from our congregation; he was with us for 7 years. Throughout that time, he was very friendly to me and my family. Now, he's going to Philadelphia. May he be happy.

It's April 8, 1947. Judy and my mother were with us for Pesach seder; however, the Slavitts were in Stamford, Connecticut. Hopefully, our celebration next year won't be any worse.

Business is good, thank God.

Leonard has gone into the real estate business.

I was at the Jewish Center, as both prayer leader and Torah reader, and it was a joyous holiday. Hopefully, we can live to celebrate next year—and Sylvia will be married.

It's April 14, 1947. I was in New York to see my Aunt Iola. She's 86 years old, but very sick.

I bought a megillah for Esther, for $36 (thank God), and a pair of brass candlesticks for $18, at a shop at 44 Eldridge Street. The money for the candlesticks was obtained by saving a little at a time.

It's April 17, 1947. Today, I bought Esther, my dear wife, a gold necklace for our 35th wedding anniversary. It cost $200. I bought it at Pincus. May she wear it in good health. She's certainly worth it. We've both worked very hard, and I hope that better times will come. Amen, Amen.

Leonard is now 30 years old, divorced, and has a 4-year-old daughter. Unfortunately, he is still living at home. And as the diary suggests, Samuel is getting concerned. "What (Leonard) plans to do in the future, I don't know. However, he's old enough to make up his own mind." Presumably, Leonard's future is now a source of conflict. Leonard needs a career to support himself and accommodate his ex-wife and daughter. Moreover, living at home with mother, father, 33-year-old sister, part-time daughter, and visiting grandmother is starting to appear strained.

Is Leonard ready to move? And more important, is Leonard well?

Leonard has been home for 7 months, after nearly 4 years in the Army. Moreover, he is still recuperating from a combat wound, hepatitis, and malaria. Accordingly, perhaps Leonard merits a longer respite.

On the other hand, Samuel may have reason to be concerned. Leonard's prospects were minimal. Moreover, he flunked out of college, failed Officers Training School, and only dabbled in business.

If Leonard's track record is any indication, Samuel had ample cause for worry. After flirting with real estate development, Leonard eventually assumed the liquor store, approximately 5 years after Samuel's death. However, while the business prospered with Samuel, it faltered with Leonard.

This "hole in the wall" store (see p. 167), filled with bottles and crates, thrived on customers who commuted to and from New York City. Called "Commuter's Liquor Store" (after Samuel's death), it bordered on the South Norwalk train station. However, as South Norwalk deteriorated, commuters went elsewhere. And unfortunately, the business, which tried relocation, eventually folded. At that time, Leonard was more than 50 years old. He never worked again and died shortly thereafter, broken in spirit and body, and without a penny to his name.

Samuel also states that he "survived an illness." Is Samuel exaggerating? Or is father like son, both disguising a serious disease? Perhaps Samuel had a mild heart attack. He was obese (5'7" and between 190 and 217 lbs.), and suffered from diabetes. Furthermore, he was chronically stressed and overworked. Finally, the illness seems related to increased religious devotion. Samuel notes that he went to the Jewish Center for "6 straight weeks"; that he is a good *ba'al tefilah;* and that with time, he will he an equally good *ba'al keriya* (capable of publicly reading the Torah). Additionally, Samuel indicates that he read the *megillah.* *Megillah* literally means "scroll," but in this context refers to the biblical "Book of Esther." This book details how Esther and Mordecai, as agents of God, saved the Jews of the Persian Empire from genocide. Thus, the "day of salvation" is celebrated as *Purim.* Furthermore, the main feature of this holiday is the public reading of the *megillah,* which was an honor bestowed upon Samuel.

Samuel also mentions a series of other holidays (*Rosh Hashana, Yom Kippur, Sukkos,* Thanksgiving, birthday, and so on). Interestingly, Judy was often present. Presumably, when Leonard returned, Judy became more entrenched within the Abramson family.

Also present during the holidays was Samuel's mother. Perhaps Samuel was more religious than his siblings, and so his home was preferred by his mother for Jewish holidays. Additionally, her presence in the home would mark four generations of Abramsons: great-grandmother, grandfather (Samuel), son (Leonard), and granddaughter (Judy), which was obviously a treat.

*   *   *

It's April 21, 1947. Aunt Ada died. She lived to the ripe old age of 86. It was a large and beautiful funeral, including two rabbis, and was held at the Memorial Chapel at 31 Canal Street.

It's April 20, 1947. Mayer Josem's wife, Ida, died. She was 63 years old. Also, Mrs. Mary Phillips died. She was Esther's grandmother from Bridgeport and was 75 years old.

It's May 4, 1947. My son and I went to see the soccer team HaPoel play in Yankee Stadium in New York. Tickets for the game cost $10 apiece.

It's May 27, 1947. Business is a little slower, but we still make about $700 a week. Furthermore, merchandise is getting cheaper, and we can get plenty of stock.

My mother was with us for Shavuos. I was in shul both days.

It's July l, 1947. Business is a bit better. May we live and be well. Also, I feel better, thank God. And, with God's help, I've been able to save money. Now, I have $3,800 in the bank, and $3,800 in war bonds. Also, I've been able to purchase $500 in war bonds for Judy.

Abe Slavitt bought a boat and took us for a ride to Long Island. We had a good time.

Sylvia is working in New York, in an office, and gets $20 a day. Also, Leonard is feeling better, thank God. May he not get any worse.

I now have $1,000 in my checking account.

Judy continues to grow into a very charming and clever young girl.

It's July 7, 1947. Congratulations. Leonard bought a Studebaker. It cost him $2,070. He put down $1,000 and will pay the remainder in monthly installments.

On Sunday we went to the New York State Park. We had a very good time.

This week business was fine, especially the 4th of July. We took in about $900, thank God.

It's July 17, 1947. We bought a dog—a boxer. A very beautiful animal. He cost $20. I love having a dog.

Business has fallen off about 35%. But I can't help it. However, I have about $1,000 in my checking account. It comes in handy when times aren't so good.

Every Sunday we go for a drive and we have a good time. We take Lance (the dog) with us and enjoy it very much. The weather is very warm.

We have plenty of stock.

It's July 22, 1947. I bought a $100 bond, bringing the total to $3,900 in government bonds.

Also, I am continuing to save, little by little, and I hope that with this money I'll be able to make a trip to the Land of Israel. It's important to me, because I don't want to be like the saying, "Shall your brethren go to war, and shall you sit here?" So, I've saved $200, and with God's help, I hope to see Israel.

It's August 21, 1947. Rabbi Tumin left for Philadelphia. May good luck and all the best go with him. He was a good friend to us.

Now, we have a new rabbi. May he be well.

It's October 27, 1947. Sylvia bought a radio. May she be well.

We were in Brooklyn for the unveiling of Chana's (my wife's sister's) monument.

Business isn't bad. However, it's hard to get liquor in the half pint, because they stopped manufacturing it for 60 days.

It's November 11, 1947. Leonard bought a washing machine for our house. It cost $257. May we use it in good health.

Fortunately, Leonard has been making good money lately. May he continue to be well.

We received $800 from the Christmas Club.

Business isn't bad, thank God. We take in $700 a week.

We went to a presentation at Lake Success. It was about the need for a Jewish state in Israel. I feel that I am fortunate to live in these times. To be able to hear the good news about the renewal of our wish for a state in Israel—and for the beginning of the redemption. Congratulations, congratulations. Thank God for all.

It's November 19, 1947. Leonard bought and sold seven parcels of land from Dr. Kahl. This land was resold at a very good price.

It's December 1, 1947. I went to New York and bought a coat from Witty Brothers for $145. Thank God for everything. The money came from the Christmas Club.

Business isn't bad.

It's December 24, 1947. Business wasn't as good as it was last year. But thank God for everything.

Rabbi Tumin is going to give Leonard a Jewish divorce, through Professor Bozkan of the Schechter Seminary.

It's January 13, 1948. Leonard was in Schechter's Seminary to finalize the papers of his Jewish divorce. I was hoping that it wouldn't come to this, but what can one do? It must've been preordained by God.

The divorce cost $50. May we not hear, or have, any more sorrow or trouble.

Samuel is torn. He wants a Jewish homeland in Israel, but is too old to fight. Moreover, he can't sit still without contributing to the cause. Thus, Samuel demands, "Shall your brethren go to war, and shall you sit here?"

This quote is derived from the Torah, "And Moshe said to the children of Gad and to the children of Re'uven, Shall your brethren go to war, and shall you sit here? (Numbers 32:6)." According to tradition, the Jewish tribes had previously wandered the desert for 40 years. Now, they were willing to fight for a homeland, and were attempting to conquer Israel. However, two tribes, Gad and Re'uven, got sidetracked. They discovered other land (East of the Jordan River) that was more suitable to cattle grazing and sought permission, from Moses, to establish a settlement.

Moses was concerned. He asked the tribes of Gad and Re'uven, "Do you intend to sit here, with your cattle, and let your brethren fight the war without you?"

"No!" assured Gad and Re'uven. "We plan to fight for Israel—but live on land for cattle."

Moses was satisfied.

Obviously, there is a parallel between Samuel's dilemma and the story of Gad and Re'uven. Both supported the fight for Israel, and both had conflicting circumstances. However, like Gad and Re'uven, Samuel also found a compromise. He contributed medical supplies to the Haganah.

Since 1920 the Haganah had been an underground Jewish defense force living in Palestine. Eventually, by 1948, the Haganah had grown to approximately 50,000 members. Therefore, the Haganah and Menachem Begin's Irgun Zvai Leumi (of approximately 2,000 members) were the primary soldiers in Israel's War of Independence.

Understandably, Samuel could not fight for the Haganah. Instead, he purchased large quantities of medical supplies (gauze, bandages, syringes, and so on), which were delivered to Israel. Paradoxically, although this was confirmed by a pharmacist who sold the supplies, Samuel does not mention this circumstance in his diary. Perhaps, like the Haganah, which was a secret organization, Samuel's war efforts also remained secret.

However, Samuel's Zionist beliefs were by no means secret. He states, in reference to Israel, "I am fortunate to live in these times." Obviously, in light of World War II, "these times" leave much to be desired. Yet, the prospect of a Jewish homeland was sufficient to rejoice for "today."

Speaking of "rejoice," this section marks Samuel's sole use of the word "love." Not coincidentally, it is in reference to his dog. Perhaps, Samuel's "love" is limited to uncomplicated affection, that of a pet, or a grandchild. If so, what does this say about Samuel? Why was he so inhibited, or emotionally blocked?

Samuel was by no means a scurrilous man. Relatives remember him as "warm and outgoing," "jolly," and "rotund." Perhaps, though he appeared "jolly" on the outside, those who knew him well (and unfortunately, are now deceased) would have portrayed a more complicated individual. Certainly, at this point in his life, Samuel was capable of enjoying a Sunday drive (in Leonard's new car) or going to a soccer game with his son. Yet, when business slowed, Samuel's "demons of blame" reappeared. However, to assuage these demons, Samuel concludes, "but I can't help it" (i.e., don't blame me).

The soccer game, by the way, was an extraordinary event. As *The New York Times* headline (May 5, 1947) indicates, "43,177 See HaPoel Soccer Team Beat New York All-Star Eleven at Stadium." This game marked the debut of a soccer team from Palestine (not yet Israel) against a "selected professional team" of 11 Americans. HaPoel won (2 to 0) as a result of "superior European style" in contrast to "inefficient" American strategy. Presumably, the soccer game was a fund-raiser for Israel's upcoming War of Independence.

Samuel also mentions a series of deaths, and the unveiling of Chana's monument. *Unveiling* refers to the consecration of the tombstone. Originally, Jews often did not use, or inscribe, monuments on the grave. However, as a result of the Diaspora, tombstones were erected and consecrated during the 12th month after death. Consecration consists of a selection of appropriate Psalms and biblical passages, concluding with a memorial prayer and *kaddish*, an ancient prayer, written primarily in Aramaic, that pays homage to God and expresses hope for God's Kingdom on Earth.

Finally, although Leonard was legally divorced, he also obtained a Jewish divorce (called a *get*). Arranged by Rabbi Tumin, the *get* is written according to rules specified in the Talmud. First, the writing materials must belong to the husband, which are then "gifted" to the "scribe," who in turn writes the divorce, based upon the husband's instructions. After the divorce is written and signed, the husband delivers the "bill of divorcement" to his wife.

Thus, Leonard obtained his *get*. At this point in the diary, Samuel also notes that Dorothy's legal name, according to Jewish tradition, was "Devorah, the daughter of Rabbi Dov Areyeh Lieb, son of Rabbi Samuel Henoch."

*   *   *

It's January 20, 1948. Leonard received his real estate license today. It wasn't difficult to earn. May he be well.

It's February 1, 1948. It was a very cold January. Fortunately, however, our house was warm. The gas bill came to $52 for the month.

Business was very good. We took in $3,000 for the month. May it not be any worse. Unfortunately, the cost of living is very expensive.

Judy is so clever and beautiful. May God protect her.

Sylvia is dating Mr. Schnabel. We are waiting to see what will materialize.

It's February 12, 1948. The stock market fell, and prices are getting cheaper. However, we don't know how long it'll last. Fortunately, business is about the same.

I am paying back an old debt to my brother-in-law (Ray's husband, Leventhal). He says that I owe him $200 and that he'll show me the bill. It annoys me that my mother never mentioned this earlier. But with God's help, I'll pay him back. If one owes, one must repay.

This winter was very cold, the coldest in 40 years. The gas bill was $60.

My sister states that 20 years ago I borrowed $200 from her and her husband. I don't remember it. If her husband insists, I will pay him. God will help.

It's March 10, 1948. I sent in the check for my state taxes—$33. However, I don't have to pay income tax until September, because I overpaid on last year's bill.

It's March 29, 1948. This Easter week, business was $200 less than last year. But one must hope for better times.

I've already repaid my brother-in-law $125 of the old debt. God will help me pay back the remainder.

It's April 5, 1948. I bought a refrigerator for the store and borrowed the money from Leonard—$700. The total cost of the refrigerator was $800. Thank God for everything.

Presently, I am saving $2 a day. And with God's help, I'll be able to pay Leonard back.

Business has gotten weaker.

Samuel is annoyed. It appears that he "forgot" an old debt, even though he views the debt with suspicion. Thus, begrudgingly, he concludes, "If one owes, one must pay."

Though Samuel made $3,000 the month before (and has more than $7,500 in savings and bonds), he makes only partial repayment ($125) of the debt, praying that "God will help me pay back the remainder." Obviously, since Samuel could afford the $75, perhaps the "unconscious message" of the prayer is "for the strength to be honest," rather than the money to pay the debt.

Also, why did Samuel borrow money from Leonard? Did he feel that Leonard owed him compensation for room and board? And if so, why not ask for assistance? Leonard is now 31 years old, working in real estate, yet living at home. Certainly, asking help from an adult son would not be inappropriate. Instead, as with the debt, Samuel acts passively, as the martyr, insolvent and beseeching God for help.

*   *   *

Following are two letters that were sent to Samuel, one from his uncle and one from a cousin:

Dear Nephew, I received your dear short letter. I thank you very much. You were always my *beoling,* even years ago. I say years ago, but what about now?

In my old age, I would still love to see you all again. I am alone. I have no one. I would yet want to see your dear mother, my beloved sister and sister-in-law. Oh, what a wonderful mother you have. May the Lord grant her many years, and what a grandmother you had—and what a grandfather!

And since we are talking about them, you wrote me once that my *yahrzeit* is 26 days in the month of Tevet. I am not sure of this because I received a letter from Noach and he wrote me that my *yahrzeit* is 26 days in *Kislav.* I don't know which is correct. Please find out for me which is the right date and let me know.

I have no more news. I am not in the best of health. My wife is sick 5 years already. It is now 3 years since I have been able to do any work. I send regards to your wife and two dear children.

I send regards to your beloved mother from the depths of my heart. Also Ada and her children and grandchildren and regards from me to Chana and her children from me. Your uncle, A. Abramson

Dear Cousin Sam, Your wish was fulfilled. My daughters went to Connecticut and visited Judy. For a two-year-old, she is simply wonderful. May God help, that her daddy will be able to take her shortly to the skating rink.

Varoshilor is leading an offensive against Japan, and the Nazis are finished, with God's help, because the Allies are on one side, and the Red Army on the other.

[can't decipher] cost 88c. I am sending the rest in stamps. You asked why I needed the ____. I take $8 from it sometimes and what remains____

Our post office is Brooklyn 13

[bottom of letter]

Write me whether you like the set ____ I am giving it to them, so that she will have something with which to play. And if you wish, I will send it to you ____ by parcel post. A second regards from ____. 4 weeks from today is Christmas. It could be that ____.

The first letter (from Samuel's mother's brother) suggests that Samuel is a valued source of family information. *Yahrzeit* (literally meaning "time of the year") refers to the anniversary of a death, commemorated according to the Hebrew calendar. Thus, Samuel's uncle is asking for clarification of the Hebrew date of an important death (either A. Abramson's father or mother). However, this is a curious request, since a grandchild (Samuel) does not observe the *yahrzeit* of his/her grandparents. Perhaps, it was assumed that Samuel would seek clarification from his mother. Finally, the letter also extols the virtues of the Abramson forebears.

The remaining letter provides additional "proof" of Samuel's devotion to Judy. Although Leonard's marriage has deteriorated, Judy is a frequent topic in Samuel's correspondence.

*   *   *

It's May 15, 1948. America has just recognized the new Jewish state of Israel. Praised be the Lord that I've lived long enough to see the rebirth of the Jewish land.

Unfortunately, war has broken out. The Arabs have attacked, but the Jews, with much strength and bravery, held out until the U.S. could arrange a cease-fire. Now, there is a 30-day truce. However, what'll happen remains to be seen. May God be our ally.

It's terrible that the Arabs have restarted a war against the Jews. Hopefully, the world powers will quickly put an end to this.

It's May 14, 1948. Congratulations, Congratulations. My daughter Sylvia became a bride-to-be. Praise the Lord. She's marrying a very fine young man, Irving Schnabel. He gave her a diamond ring—1-1/2 carats. I pray to God, that they'll have a happy life together.

It's May 24, 1948. Congratulations, Congratulations. My son Leonard gave Ethel Sakowitz a diamond ring. May it bring good wishes. Amen, Amen. May God grant him health and happiness with her.

If one lives long enough, one will see the triumph of good. I didn't think that all these wonderful events would happen so soon—and I pray to God that it'll work out well.

It's about time that our devoted children have gotten happiness. God should repay them for all their goodness. Amen, Amen.

It's May 23, 1948. Sunday was our wedding anniversary. We went to a Jewish play in New York. We also dined at my in-laws, and had another meal downtown. And for a present, I bought Esther a string of pearls. May we be healthy and have joy from our children.

It's June 2, 1948. We're waiting impatiently for the happy day of our daughter's wedding. May they have good luck. Amen, Amen. I will give her $200 as a wedding present. She can buy herself a set of silverware. May she use it in good health. If one lives long enough, one will eventually see some good.

I think my wife Esther will also give Sylvia a wedding present, probably a silver set.

It was raining, but we had company. Sylvia, her fiancé Irving, Leonard, and his friend Clarence Abramson. We all had a very good time.

Business isn't bad. May we all be well. God will help.

It's June 4, 1948. I was in the government hospital. My eyes were bothering me, so Abraham took me to have my eyes examined.

Dr. Schneider examined my eyes, and requested that I come for several appointments, so that he can check me out. I hope my eyes will get better.

On June 12, I spent the day in the hospital. My eyes were clear and okay.

It's June 14, 1948. Sylvia had a surprise party. She received a set of china, plus other presents. Her mother gave her a set of silver. May she use it in good health. Amen. Amen.

Leonard bought a wristwatch for Ethel. May she use it in good health. Thank God for all.

Thank God for everything. May we have pleasure from our children. Amen, Amen.

It's June 20, 1948. Congratulations, congratulations. We were invited to our children's engagement party. It was lovely, and we had a good time. May they enjoy many years of health and prosperity.

We gave her a present.

It's June 22, 1948. I bought Sylvia a good wool blanket for her birthday. It cost $20. May she use it in good health. I also gave her $200 in cash to buy a sterling silver set. May she use it with much happiness. Amen, Amen.

My Esther also bought Sylvia a silver set—for $80. May she use it in good health. She certainly deserves it all. Thank God, my eyes have witnessed this, and that I have money for everything.

Esther gave Sylvia a third set of silver. Originally, the silver belonged to Esther: I'd bought it as a 25th anniversary present. So now Sylvia has three sets of silver. May she use them in good health.

Sylvia's cousin from Pennsylvania also sent her a set of silverware, making four sets in all. Praise the Lord.

It's July 14, 1948. Sylvia emptied a closet in her bedroom. She plans to go away to get married. Let it be with good health. I hope they will always be with me, but one never knows what time will bring.

It's September 1, 1948. Leonard's girlfriend was a bit insulted when Sylvia told her not to come to the house every night. So, she left in a huff. We're waiting to see what'll happen. The bottom line is that Leonard can't get married. He doesn't earn enough. May God help him find a way to make a living for himself.

Business is poor.

It was 103 degrees on September l, but now it's became cooler.

Sylvia has settled into the house. Her husband is a fine young man.

It's September 10, 1948. Sylvia went back to work as a teacher. She now receives $4,000 a year. Irving also earns a good salary. May God help them.

Abe Slavitt got a car for Sylvia—a Chevrolet. It cost $1,675. May she use the car in good health.

Business isn't bad. There is plenty of stock, and it doesn't take much work.

Praise God for everything that my eyes have witnessed, and that I've lived to experience this joy. Amen, Amen.

It's September 19, 1948. I was in Brooklyn, at the bar mitzvah of Martin Leventhal's son. We drove in with Sylvia and her husband, and we all had a good time.

While in New York, we also visited my cousin Yechiel. They served a very good supper, played music, and we all enjoyed ourselves.

On Sunday we visited Schnabel's sister, and enjoyed ourselves very much.

My daughter stayed at Irving's family's house. May she have a good future. Amen, Amen.

It's October 12, 1948. May God give us a good New Year.

Everything is the same. My son-in-law and daughter were a bit angry with Leonard and Ethel. I can't understand what they want from Ethel. She's a fine girl, and this bickering makes us sick in our hearts. My wife can't stand it.

In the meantime, Ethel doesn't come to see us. Or if she does come, she won't speak to Sylvia. It's terribly upsetting to me. What the future will bring, I don't know.

Business isn't bad, but won't be as good as it once was.

Surprisingly, this is the first mention of my (Paul Abramson's) mother, Ethel Sakowitz. Obviously, Samuel knew Ethel prior to Leonard's engagement. In fact, Samuel introduced Ethel to Leonard.

On March 5, 1947, Samuel's diary contains the following sentence: "Thank God for everything—that I am still here and that I was able to survive my illness." That "illness" was a benign prostatic hypertrophy (i.e., an enlarged prostate), with bladder outlet obstruction. Although frightening, Samuel's illness was not life-threatening.

Samuel was treated at Norwalk Hospital. And as fate would have it, Ethel Sakowitz was his nurse. Furthermore, Ethel was single, finishing her bachelor's degree at New York University, and recently discharged (as a lieutenant) from the Army. Supposedly, Samuel told Ethel, "I know someone for you!"

Leonard and Ethel were a "hit." And not surprisingly, Samuel and Esther were delighted. Ethel was an extraordinary young woman. At 25 years of age, she held a professional degree, she was an officer in the Army, a veteran of World War II, one of the few Jewish women to enlist in the Army (and then to use the GI Bill for a college education), and was nearly finished with her bachelor's degree at NYU. Paradoxically, Ethel had achieved everything that Leonard had not.

Thus, why isn't Ethel mentioned prior to her engagement? All of Sylvia's suitors are duly noted. And furthermore, Ethel was already "part of the family," attending dinners and making short trips with Leonard, Esther, and Samuel. (She went to New York on December 1, 1947, when Samuel "bought a coat from Witty Brothers.")

Perhaps, by this time, Samuel was losing faith, and had tired of Leonard's disappointments. Maybe Samuel felt that he should take a wait-and-see attitude. However, this doesn't seem like Samuel, the man who worries about everything.

More likely, Samuel was being overly cautious (and superstitious), so as not to jinx this relationship. Furthermore, despite Samuel's acceptance of Ethel, her courtship with Leonard had the potential of jeopardizing Samuel's relationship with Judy. Ethel was not thrilled with Judy nor with the intricacies of Leonard's prior marriage and divorce. Therefore, if Leonard and Ethel are "for real,"

Samuel would have the consolation of future grandchildren, within an intact couple. However, if Leonard and Ethel were "for naught," Judy's status would remain the same—a favored grandchild, with a questionable future within the Abramson family.

However, once the engagement was official, Ethel was finally recognized in the diary. Besides Samuel's written commentary, he included the following newspaper reports of the engagement:

FORMER ARMY NURSE ENGAGED

Mr. and Mrs. Samuel Sakowitz of 279 Cleveland Avenue announce the engagement of their daughter, Ethel Esther, to Leonard Abramson, son of Mr. and Mrs. Samuel Abramson of 5 Cedar Street, South Norwalk.

Miss Sakowitz is a graduate of Bassick High School and the Norwalk General Hospital School of Nursing. She is a senior at New York University. During the war she served as a first lieutenant in the Army nurse corps, and was stationed in the Philippine Islands. Mr. Abramson served in the 32nd Red Arrow division of the U.S. Army. He is a real estate broker.

TO WED IN NEW YORK

A license to wed was obtained at the Municipal Building here Thursday by Miss Ethel E. Sakowitz, R.N., 26, of 279 Cleveland Avenue, Bridgeport, and Leonard Abramson, 32, of 5 Cedar Street, Norwalk, Connecticut.

The couple said they would be married in New York on January 30.

Miss Sakowitz was born in Bridgeport, the daughter of Samuel and Anna Hartman Sakowitz. Her prospective husband, the son of Samuel and Esther Abramson, was born in Norwalk.

Yet, despite the newspaper highlights, there is still a conspicuous lack of details about Ethel in the diary. "She's a fine girl" is about all that Samuel conveys at this point. In contrast, Irving Schnabel is a "very fine young man" . . . (who) "earns a good salary." Obviously, Ethel also earned a good salary, in addition to being an Army officer and a (soon to be) college graduate. Irving, by the way, never attended college, and was a furrier by trade—two facts that Samuel never mentions.

It is interesting to note that I (Paul Abramson) always assumed that Irving was an attorney (I have other uncles who are lawyers). It wasn't until I was 22 years old that I learned his true occupation. Surprisingly (or, given my family, not surprisingly), nobody ever mentioned Irving's job, even though Irving and Sylvia lived in Norwalk, and we often visited during the holidays.

Also not surprising is Samuel's sexist disregard of Ethel's educational and economic achievements. Men of his generation were often indifferent to the accomplishments of women. Yet, Samuel's sexism is not unidimensional. His daughter is a college graduate and works as a teacher. Perhaps, Samuel's attitude toward the accomplishments of women is compartmentalized into two categories: before and after marriage. Education has intrinsic value and facilitates a women's status prior to marriage. However, after marriage, what matters is a woman's "character" and her work within the home. Not surprisingly, my father (Leonard) shared this belief. He refused to allow my mother to work, despite his repeated business failures and economic straits. On the other hand, his attitude and its consequence (my mother did not work between 1949 and 1974) say as much about my mother as about my father. (In defense of my father, my mother states that despite his attitude [and their many economic problems], she preferred to stay at home with her children. However, if she were young and married in the 1980s, she now states, she would combine her career with her family. Finally, following my father's death in 1975, my mother continued working as a nurse until 1987, when she retired just prior to her 65th birthday.)

Interestingly, despite recognition of Sylvia's engagement to Irving, there is no mention of their marriage. Obviously, they got married, and Samuel refers to Irving as his son-in-law. Thus, where was the marriage? And why doesn't Samuel mention his reactions to this circumstance?

Sylvia and Irving eloped. Family legend indicates that Sylvia felt pressured by the prospect of being upstaged by Leonard's second marriage, so they hastily eloped. However, it is not clear whether this represents the entire reason. Sylvia was 35 years old, and perhaps a "bird in the hand" warranted hasty measures. Also, perhaps there was something about Sylvia and Samuel's relationship (i.e. [I hope she] "will always be with me—but one never knows") that made it difficult for her to get married in his presence. Conceivably, she (and Irving) wanted to avoid the turmoil of a traditional wedding, so they eloped. Finally, since Leonard and Dorothy tried to elope to hide a premarital pregnancy, this possibility also exists. However, this latter prospect is unlikely, unless a miscarriage occurred, since Sylvia and Irving waited several years before having a child.

Why doesn't Samuel mention his reactions to Sylvia's elopement? Perhaps, he feared the worst (a pregnancy), and didn't want to acknowledge the fact. Also, given his fears about Sylvia's future, he may have accepted any marriage ceremony, and felt no reason to dwell upon it.

After Sylvia and Irving were married, they moved into Samuel and Esther's home. As the diary indicates, the home got crowded, and the young couples fought. Furthermore, with Judy present on weekends, there must have been considerable tension for all.

Despite the bickering, Samuel is obviously relishing these times. He is delighted that his children are getting married and he is enjoying the excitement. Thus, although Samuel is having eye problems (presumably, as a result of his diabetes), he has finally "lived long enough" for happiness to occur. Moreover, this happiness has come at a time when Samuel is financially stable and is able to contribute to the festivities.

Finally, Samuel has also "lived long enough" to see a cherished religious goal, statehood for Israel, which was declared on May 14, 1948. On the following day, British troops and administration withdrew from the country. However, as Samuel indicates, all was not well with Israel. Although the United States officially recognized the Jewish

State on May 15, 1948, the Arab nations (Lebanon, Syria, Iraq, Transjordan, and Egypt) attacked Israel in protest. Furthermore, despite a United Nations resolution on May 22, which called for a cease-fire within 36 hours, the fighting persisted.

*   *   *

It's October 11, 1948. This house was originally bought in Sylvia's name. Now Sylvia turned the ownership over to me. However, when I die, the house will go to Esther. And when we are both dead, the house will belong to Sylvia.

If the house becomes Esther's, she may do whatever she wants with it. She worked just as hard for the money as I did.

It's November 22, 1948. Business has fallen off, but we continue to make a living.

The quarrel is continuing. My son-in-law doesn't talk to my future daughter-in-law. Also, we were going to have a Thanksgiving dinner, but instead, Leonard is going to Bridgeport, which annoys Sylvia. So, we'll have a small dinner at home.

This is the 21st day in Chesvan, and I turned 64 years old. Thank God that we've lived this long, and may our life be better as time goes on.

It's December 2, 1948. I was in New York City, where I bought two suits for myself with money I received from the Christmas Club. I paid $82 for the two suits. Now I have enough things to wear, except that I want to buy a corduroy jacket and pay about $20.

Thank God business isn't bad.

Esther began saving $5 a week in the Christmas Club.

It's December 27, 1948. This past Saturday was Christmas, and I was able to rest for 2 days.

Business, thank God, was like last year. And fortunately, we had plenty of stock. In fact, on December 24 we took in $700. And for this week we took in $1,200, which is very satisfactory.

May we be well, and thank God for all.

Leonard is preparing to get married. May it be with good luck. Amen, Amen.

It's January 6, 1949. Business isn't bad. I have, thank God, $1,600 in cash in the bank. And from my checking account, I have enough to pay off the Frigidaire.

Paid back Lennie $700. Also, the floor and painting cost over $1,000. Praise God, I paid it off.

It's January 27, 1949. We were in Bridgeport Sunday. Ethel's parents had a party for the children. They're going to be married on Sunday, January 30, 1949. May it be with good luck, and in a lucky hour.

I gave Leonard a present of $100. May he use it in good health.

Leonard and Ethel are going to live in Houston, Texas.

It's January 30, 1949. Leonard and Ethel are going on a 2-week honeymoon to Florida. May God be with them.

Ethel got a job as head nurse in a hospital in Houston. It hurts me that my son is leaving this area. But I can't hold my children with me forever.

Let Leonard try his luck there, and may God grant him good health and success. Also, may God give me continued good health, so that I can work and make some money for my old age.

Age is gradually creeping up on me, and one has to have the dollar. Money is a person's best friend.

Ethel's parents gave them a $500 present. May they use it in good health. They also received several other fine gifts. In fact, my mother gave them a pair of silver candlesticks. May they use it all in good health.

As Samuel indicates, the "children" are still fighting. Perhaps, since the house was in Sylvia's name, she demanded preferential treatment within the home. However, it is never clear why the home needed to be in Sylvia's name in the first place. And furthermore, why is it now turned over to Samuel?

Attached to the diary is a newspaper article listing the quitclaim deeds for October 11, 1948. Among the entries are two for Samuel and Sylvia:

Saul (sic) Abramson et ux to Sylvia A. Schnabel, Cedar St.
Sylvia A. Schnabel to Saul (sic) Abramson et ux, Cedar St.

A quitclaim deed represents that one person (grantor) is conveying a title or interest to another person (grantee). However, it does not warrant that the title or interest is actually owned by the grantor. Thus, these entries suggest that Samuel gave title to Sylvia, who in turn, gave it back to him. However, it is unclear whether the title was ever truly given to Sylvia. Furthermore, why were the two exchanges recorded on the same day? Presumably, the initial title was several years old. Finally, why is title given back to Samuel after Sylvia's marriage? Was title to the house (perhaps in name only) a further inducement to keep Sylvia at home. And now that she is married, did Samuel symbolically retransfer the title?

Also confusing is the fact that Samuel waited until now to repay Leonard for the refrigerator and compensate him for painting the house. Obviously, Samuel could well afford to have repaid Leonard earlier. Perhaps, Samuel (and Esther) were unconsciously perpetuating Leonard's dependence. On the other hand, it is also conceivable that Samuel did not trust Leonard, and as such, waited until Leonard was ready to marry (hence, become responsible) before repaying him.

But eventually, Leonard escaped through the urging of his new wife. Ethel noted a job advertisement in *The New York Times,* for a Head Nurse at Hermann Hospital in Houston, Texas. It paid well and, to her delight, she received the position. Paradoxically, it was the only job she applied for. She wanted to start anew and be away from the stifling effect of Leonard's parents.

Although Samuel is continuing to enjoy some of his circumstances (appreciating his wife, buying himself clothes), his pessimistic resignation is settling back in ("business falling off . . . we make a living"; "may our life be better as time goes on"; "I can't hold my children with me forever"). Worse yet, Samuel concludes that "money is a person's best friend." This comment perhaps symbolizes the tragedy of Samuel's life. He doesn't have close friends; he doesn't appreciate love and intimacy; and he is overly attached to his material possessions, which, unfortunately, given his psychology, are never plentiful nor stable enough. Furthermore, it appears that his feelings about money are inextricably bound to his feelings about age and death. Perhaps he believes that if he has enough money, he will be able to compensate for (or banish) the fear and torment of impending death. Last, at no point does Samuel express that he has been content with his life. Instead, he views his life as a succession of mishaps and mistakes—with transient moments of pleasure.

*   *   *

It's January 30, 1949. Congratulations, Leonard is married. May the hour be fortuitous. He's certainly worth all the best and it's about time he got some happiness.

The ceremony took place in the Spanish Portuguese synagogue in New York. Afterwards, we went to dinner at the Paramount Restaurant and had a wonderful time. My mother, Jennie and Abe Slavitt, and Chana and her husband were also there, and the weather was fine. May we hear only good things from Leonard. Amen, Amen.

It's February 12, 1949. Two weeks have passed since Leonard and Ethel left on their honeymoon. He was in Washington and enjoyed himself very much. But now we haven't heard from him in a week and we don't receive any letters. He's presumably in Saint Augustine, Florida, visiting his old friend Snyder.

Presently, it's hard for me to work alone in the store. But there is nothing I can do. Leonard must make a living for himself. That's what happens after you bring up your children. As one gets older, the children fly away from you. And as old age comes upon you, you are left to fend for yourself. May God grant me health, so that I can take care of myself.

We received pictures from Leonard. He's having a good time.

It's February 21, 1949. We received a letter from Leonard today. He states that he'll be in Texas next week. I hope to hear good news from him.

I now have $4,900 in government bonds. Please God, let me save $100 toward another bond.

It's March 7, 1949. We receive letters from Leonard. Ethel has started her job, and Leonard is looking for one. They already have an apartment, and Leonard's rent is $100 per month. Time will tell how things will work out for them. Fortunately, we receive frequent letters from them.

May God help them.

It's March 15, 1949. Purim was March 14, and I read the megillah at the Jewish Center. Everything was well arranged. May we live to celebrate this again next year.

We receive frequent letters from Leonard. At the moment, he's unemployed. I hope he'll find something soon and earn a living for himself.

It's March 26, 1949. We continue to receive frequent letters from Leonard.

Business slowed down a bit. But one can still make a living, thank God. Today I purchased a bond. This comes to $5,000 in government bonds. Let this money be for my wife, to cover her in her old age. She worked very hard for it too.

It's April 18, 1949. My mother joined us for Pesach seder—may she live long. It was a joyous occasion. However, we missed Leonard and his wife.

Leonard called us today on the telephone. They're satisfied to be living in Texas.

Business is a bit weaker, but we make a living. Thank God for everything.

It's May 12, 1949. Praise God—Israel became a member of the United Nations, and was accepted with a majority of 37 votes. Today, at 9:30 A.M., the Jewish flag will fly at the United Nations building. And at last we have a Jewish state. Praise the Lord.

I received a letter from Leonard today. He's leaving Houston next week. Thank God for everything. May he come home well.

It's May 20, 1949. Leonard and Ethel left Texas today. May they arrive home well.

The diary contains the following newspaper article about Leonard and Ethel's wedding:

ABRAMSON-SAKOWITZ NUPTIALS TOOK PLACE IN N.Y. SYNAGOGUE

Of interest here is the marriage of Leonard Abramson, former Norwalk real estate operator, and Miss Ethel E. Sakowitz, R.N., daughter of Mr. and Mrs. Samuel Sakowitz of 279 Cleveland Street, Bridgeport, which took place Sunday at 2 P.M. in the Spanish Portuguese-American synagogue in New York City.

Rabbi Desola Pool officiated at the ceremony, which was followed by a dinner in the Paramount Restaurant.

The bride chose a two-piece frock of gold brocade fashioned with long sleeves and a peplum. Her cafe au lait straw hat was tied under the chin with veiling and her accessories matched. She wore white orchids.

The couple were unattended.

Both young people are war veterans and served in the Philippines. Mrs. Abramson served in the Army Nurse Corps and recently was graduated in nursing education from New York University. She has been a staff duty nurse at Norwalk Hospital.

Mr. Abramson, son of Mr. and Mrs. Samuel Abramson of 5 Cedar Street, this city, served in the infantry.

After a honeymoon in Florida, for which the bride changed to a tangerine tone wool suit with navy blue accessories for traveling, the couple will take up residence in Houston, Texas.

Mrs. Abramson will become associated with a hospital in Houston and Mr. Abramson will enter the real estate business there.

Prior to the wedding, the bride was given a surprise shower at her home in Bridgeport by staff duty and private duty nurses of the Norwalk Hospital.

As the diary indicates, the wedding was followed by a honeymoon in Florida. Perhaps not surprisingly, Samuel is already starting to complain. Even on his honeymoon, Leonard (who is now 33 years old) is expected to maintain close contact with his parents.

Obviously, Samuel is having great difficulty letting go of his son. While the family has never emphasized individuation, Samuel's symbiosis appears to be increasing. He is lonely, and perhaps afraid of dying. Thus, Leonard's presence would diminish his loneliness (at home and in the store) as well as minimize Samuel's fears of penury, which perhaps mask his fears of death. Note how Samuel unabashedly thanks God that Leonard is leaving Houston. No mention is made of Ethel, nor Ethel's pregnancy, which was the ostensible reason for leaving. Conceivably, if Leonard were also gainfully employed, there would have been less pressing need to leave Texas. Instead, Leonard was unemployed and, with the prospects of a new family, decided to head home.

Of course, Leonard did not have a flourishing career in Connecticut, either. He occasionally sold some real estate, and worked in his father's store. Presumably, the real estate options in Houston were as viable as those in Connecticut. Thus, why the rush home? Perhaps, Leonard had no intention (i.e., unconsciously) of staying in Texas, and only half-heartedly sought employment. Obviously, once Ethel became pregnant, he would have to support the family, which meant returning to his "home base". Thus, Leonard could allow Ethel to do whatever she wanted until she became pregnant, which would necessarily force them back to Connecticut. And as time would tell, Leonard would become entrenched in his father's store, fulfilling his father's dreams and his wife's fears.

Once back in Connecticut, Leonard and Ethel moved into Samuel and Esther's home, rejoining Sylvia and Irving. Presumably, this was *not* "one big happy family."

However, it is interesting to note that although Samuel laments the departure of his children, he is really talking about Leonard. Sylvia has stayed put and gives no evidence of straying far. Irving also seems content with his locale, if not his immediate surroundings. Furthermore, to what extent did Samuel (and Esther) blame Ethel? Obviously, the trip to Texas was inspired by Ethel's opportunities, not Leonard's. Although Samuel does not disparage Ethel in the diary, he doesn't go to great lengths to praise her, either. Ethel, in turn, remembers Samuel as a very talkative man with a good sense of humor. Though he never expressed anger, she remembers him as constantly worrying.

Finally, on May 12, 1949, Samuel mentions that Israel became a member of the United Nations. Originally, Israel applied for admission to the United Nations in November 1948. However, the Security Council did not endorse Israel's application. When Israel applied again, in February 1949, the Security Council reversed its vote and endorsed the recommendation. Thus, after considerable debate, the General Assembly finally accepted Israel on May 11, 1949.

*   *   *

Business is weak. There's been a beer strike for 8 weeks, but fortunately, I still have plenty of beer.

It's May 24, 1949. Leonard and his wife arrived home today at 10 a.m. It took 4 days, and they had a pleasant trip. I hope he'll be able to find something to do here.

Business is poor. The store makes about $500 a week without beer. One hopes that this'll improve over time.

My wife and I are very pleased. We went to a wedding in Waterbury, 26 miles away. I bought the bride and groom a silver bread tray, and Sylvia bought them a silver brush. May they use it in good health.

I contributed 18 quarters and Esther contributed 4 quarters to the Israel box. May they live and be well.

It's June 16, 1949. Leonard is still living with us, but Sylvia is unhappy. Unfortunately, it's difficult for him to get an apartment. Perhaps, he will end up building his own house. But in the meantime, they're both still with me, thank God.

Business is about the same. One makes a living.

Bobby Slavitt (Abe and Jennie's son) graduated college. There was a write-up in the newspaper on June 15. He's a very fine boy.

It's June 22, 1949. Leonard has begun building his house. It's on one of his lots, on Colony Street in Norwalk. Now, he's trying to get a mortgage.

It's June 27, 1949. My brother-in-law (Abe Slavitt) made out my will. After my death, everything that I possess will go to my beloved wife Esther. After Esther's death, the house will go to Sylvia, but the bonds and the store will go to Leonard. However, as long as Esther is alive, she has the authority to do as she wishes. Also, I'll buy a plot and pick out a stone in the cemetery.

The witness for this will was the office girl who worked for Max Raskin and Robert Goodman.

It's July 13, 1949. There's still trouble between Leonard and Irving. They don't get along, and I can't stand it. My well-being is greatly affected by it. But, may they both be well.

Webb, the architect, drew up a plan for a four-room bungalow that Leonard is going to build. May he have good luck.

Business became quite poor. But with God's help, it'll pick up again.

It's August 5, 1949. It's been very difficult for Leonard to obtain a mortgage for the house. In the meantime, they live with me. May the good Lord help him.

It's September 3, 1949. It was a very hot summer, but now it's cooler, thank God.

There wasn't much work. But God will help.

Leonard's wife caught a draft in her face, and we're very worried about her. We hope she'll be better. In the meantime, worries abound.

It's September 12, 1949. Sarah Josem, Mendel's wife, died. She was sick for a month, and now she is buried in the Lodge Cemetery. It was a large funeral.

Leonard received an appraisal from the government, on a VA loan. I hope he'll begin building shortly.

It's September 19, 1949. Leonard began digging the foundation for his house. Amen. Thank God for everything.

It's September 26, 1949. On this Rosh Hashanah, we prayed in the new temple. It was very nice.

My mother doesn't feel well. She fell down the stairs, and was taken to the hospital. They took an X ray and, thank God, she didn't break anything. However, now she is lying in bed. She had a heart attack, but it was a light one. We hope she'll be well soon.

It's September 28, 1949. Leonard started building his house. May it be with luck. He also received a $750 commission, from the land in Westport that he purchased with Dr. Margold. He hopes to do well. Amen.

It's October 7, 1949. The foundation is finished and the construction is about to begin.

It's October 13, 1949. We had company. Aaron Snyder, from Florida, was with us for 4 days, and we had a good time. Everything is okay.

Leonard is building his house, and we hope he'll have a home of his own shortly. Thank God for everything.

The carpenter's work is going well.

My mother is in bed with a cracked ankle, from her fall. Her foot is in a cast. May God help her achieve a quick cure.

It's October 20, 1949. Leonard's house is still in the process of construction. He started it on October 7, 1949. Presently, the frame and the chimney are complete. Fortunately, the weather has also been good.

Leonard works very hard—by himself—and may God help him. I gave a bottle of good whiskey to the roofer, and the outside is already finished. Now, they are starting on the interior.

It's October 26, 1949. The plumbing and fireplace are now being installed. Also, the shingles are being put on the roof.

I bought them a set of brass for their fireplace, which cost $32. May they use it in good health.

The house is now being painted. The painters are charging $100; however, the paint itself will cost about $65. It should be a good job.

It's November 4, 1949. Leonard's house looks very good. The electrical system is now being installed, and they're also working on the walls. It won't be long before it's done.

It's November 14, 1949. The electricity and wiring are now installed. They're also plastering the interior walls. It won't be long before Leonard will have his own home. God helps.

It's November 26, 1949. The plastering is now completed, and the windows and doors are in. In a couple of weeks Leonard will have—with God's help—a house of his own.

It's December 13, 1949. The floors are now laid, and in a few more days, the carpets, the locks, and the trimming will be finished. Now, may God help him earn a living. Amen, Amen.

Not surprisingly, the Abramson household has been in turmoil. After leisurely driving home from Texas, Leonard and Ethel (and their dog Texy) joined Samuel (and his dog Lance), Esther, Sylvia, and Irving. Furthermore, this is not a group of children. Excepting Ethel, the rest are considerably more than 30 years old. Finally, adding to the complications, Ethel is pregnant. Incidentally, after Ethel and Leonard returned to Samuel's home, Judy's visits to the home ceased. Conceivably, Judy was an additional "hidden issue," that is, a further source of conflict among Ethel, Leonard, and Samuel.

Disregarding the severity of the problem, Samuel states (referring to Sylvia and Leonard), "they're both still with me, thank God." Presumably, Samuel was capable of ignoring the significance of the turmoil as long as he could continue to maintain control of his children. One wonders why Sylvia and Irving did not move out, given that both were successfully employed. While buying a house may not have been feasible, renting an apartment would have certainly been an advantage over the current circumstances. Perhaps Sylvia resented the possibility of being displaced on account of Leonard and Ethel, so she refused to move. Leonard, on the other hand, could neither afford an apartment nor qualify for a conventional loan, since he was not regularly employed.

How much money did Leonard have? Obviously, if Leonard owned real estate lots, he certainly had viable assets. With a VA loan, Leonard was able to build a home on Colony Street (supplemented by his own labor/construction skills). Furthermore, over the next several years, Leonard attempted to develop other residential lots, but failed (for one reason or another) to see the projects to fruition. Perhaps if Leonard sold some of his land, the financial gain would still be insufficient to establish his independence (i.e., rent an apartment). However, despite the absence of regular employment, Leonard still had "potential" for development. Yet, both he and Sylvia chose to stay with their parents (and each other).

Also, what was Leonard's role in the store? Throughout my youth, I (Paul Abramson) remember hearing that my father was "helping out at the store." Yet, since when does an unemployed man in his mid-thirties "help out" in a store without receiving regular compensation? It was never the case that Leonard was employed by his father, or had entered into joint partnership. Instead, Leonard worked every night in the store, and during the day, as well, when he wasn't otherwise occupied. Was Samuel so selfish (or manipulative or afraid) to join in partnership with his son? Or was Leonard's supposed "compensation" provided in Samuel's will, that is, title to the store? Certainly, a 33-year-old man can spend his time more profitably than waiting for the inheritance of a liquor store. And furthermore, Samuel's strategy, and perhaps Leonard's collusion, says as much about the father as about the son.

In Samuel's classic form of understatement, he mentions that Ethel caught a "draft in the face." In reality, Ethel suffered from Bell's palsy, which is an idiopathic unilateral facial paralysis. Although Ethel had a complete recovery within several months, Bell's palsy is occasionally irreversible, especially if nerve damage has occurred. Interestingly, the cause of Bell's palsy is unknown. *The Merck Manual* indicates that the "underlying mechanism is presumed to involve swelling of the nerve due to immune or viral disease, with ischemia and compression of the facial nerve in the narrow confines of its course through the temporal bone." However, given the family turmoil, I (Paul Abramson) can't help but wonder to what extent the Bell's palsy was generated by psychological factors. Moreover, even if Bell's palsy is not psychogenic in nature, stress can reduce immune efficiency, which would indirectly affect the course of this disease. Finally, I was shocked and upset that my mother suffered facial paralysis during her pregnancy with me. She was obviously vulnerable and didn't need added complications.

Undoubtedly, Samuel was not immune to all the crises, since he mentions that "worries abound." Furthermore, his aging mother had an accident. At first, Samuel indicates that nothing was broken, but later, in passing, mentions that her ankle is "cracked." Is this another instance of Samuel's attempt to minimize an illness—or was the bone only partially "cracked"?

As usual, Samuel seeks solace in God. He indicates that the Conservative congregation now has its own temple. Incidentally, only Conservative and Reform Jews utilize the word "temple." In contrast, Orthodox Jews refer to their place of worship as a synagogue, or *shul* (from the Yiddish). According to Orthodox tradition, there is only one Temple site, located in Jerusalem, and that site has not been occupied since the last Temple was destroyed in 70 C.E.

Last, Samuel duly notes the construction of Leonard's home. In his compulsive manner, Samuel records the date each section is completed and the cost, if known. Samuel also makes his own contribution—whiskey to the roofer and brass for the fireplace. However, despite mentioning that Leonard is working "very hard," there is very little humanity in Samuel's meticulous documentation. Is Samuel proud of Leonard? Is Samuel happy that Leonard is moving out (and only 2 miles away)? Unfortunately, nothing emotional is recorded, except Samuel's obsessions over the progress of the "small bungalow," which, of course, are testimony in themselves.

*   *   *

Any day now, Leonard's wife expects to go to the hospital. May God help her to give birth without complications.

Leonard has, thank God, a home. If one lives long enough, one will see good.

It's December 14, 1949. On the 3rd week of Cheshvan, I turned 65 years old. Thank God, I don't feel bad, and may the future not be any worse.

Business is a little better. May we only be well.

My mother is still in bed.

It's December 18, 1949. My mother is still in bed. They took an X ray of her foot, and finally it's better.

Business is slow, though it'll probably pick up again.

It's December 23, 1949. On Friday, at 2 A.M., my daughter-in-law Ethel left for the hospital. And with God's help, she gave birth to a son. He's a lovely baby, weighing 7 pounds, 8 ounces. May she bring him up to be a healthy child.

The child was born Saturday, Shabbos—the 4th of Teveth. He was 21-1/2 inches long. His Jewish name is Yakov Zalmon, and his English name is Paul Richard.

It's December 31, 1949. Paul's bris was Shabbos, December 31. Dr. Weinstein was the mohel, and Rabbi Schwartz was also there. May this be a fortunate hour. Amen.

As the diary indicates, I (Paul Abramson) was born on December 24th, 1949. It is a rather unusual day for a birthday, since it is always upstaged by Christmas.

My Jewish name is *Yakov Zalmon. Yakov* is one of the three "fathers" of Judaism (Avraham, Yitzhak, and Yakov). Each "father" was said to have embodied a particular attribute: Avraham was known for his great kindness, Yitzhak for his sense of justice, and Yakov for his commitment to truth.

Interestingly, though I never knew my Jewish name prior to reading this diary, I have always conceived my higher purpose as the "quest for truth." Even as a child, this was a vaguely evident force. Perhaps, since secrets were pervasive within my family, I was driven to unravel fabrications. However, as I grew older, and confronted universal secrets, my quest was undoubtedly translated into a desire to become a psychologist. Thus, family secrets are perhaps now synonymous with the psychological mysteries that I attempt to resolve.

Eight days after birth, I had my *bris,* which literally means "covenant," and is an abbreviation for *bris mila,* the covenant of circumcision. Jewish circumcision supposedly originated when God told Abraham (who was 99 years old) to circumcise himself. According to Jewish tradition, God commanded: "Every male among you shall be circumcised. And ye shall be circumcised in the flesh of your foreskin, and it shall be a token of a covenant betwixt Me and you. And he that is eight days old shall be circumcised among you, every male throughout your generations" (Gen. 17: 11-12).

The *bris* ritual proceeds as follows. The godmother takes the child from the mother, and hands him (at the door of the room) to the godfather. The godfather, in turn, hands the child to the *mohel* (circumcisor). The *mohel* briefly places the child on the "Chair of Elijah" and then places the child on a pillow, which is resting on the knees of the *sandak.* The *sandak,* by tradition, is the most religious person known to the parents. Thus, the *sandak* hold's the baby's legs, while the *mohel* performs the circumcision.

When the circumcision is complete, the child's father recites the following benediction: "Who hast hallowed us to make our sons enter into the covenant of Abraham our father." In turn, the remaining guests reply, "Even as this child has entered into the covenant, so may he enter into the Torah, the marriage canopy, and into good deeds."

Following the benediction, the child is returned to the father (or an honored guest). Subsequently, the *mohel* (holding a glass of wine) recites two additional benedictions, one for the wine, and one for God, who established a covenant with His people, Israel. The *mohel* then recites a prayer for the welfare of the child, during the course of which the name of the child is announced. Finally, the *mohel* allows the child to drink a few drops of wine, which is succeeded by a festive meal for those present.

Circumcision has considerable symbolic value within the Jewish religion. It is meant to heighten an awareness of God and sanctify the human body, as a reminder to use one's body for holy purposes.

Finally, in order to insure the proficiency of circumcision, the *mohel* receives considerable training in both disinfection and surgical technique. However, despite rabbinic recognition, the *mohel* is usually not a physician. Nevertheless, in my case, the *bris* was performed by a physician (Dr. Weinstein, who was my mother's anesthesiologist) within a hospital setting.

Samuel also notes that Rabbi Schwartz attended my *bris*. Rabbi Schwartz was the new rabbi for Temple Beth El. Interestingly, after more than 20 years at Temple Beth El, Rabbi Schwartz resigned, to teach psychology at a local community college.

*   *   *

It's January 16, 1950. Dr. Skluth opened an office near us. May he be successful.

Business has slackened off. I now do about $500 a week. Eventually, however, I believe that it'll be better.

Leonard's house is now finished. I hope he'll move in (with my best wishes) this week. Praise God for all.

It's January 19th, 1950. Today, Mr. Harris left for Israel. May he return in good health.

Dear God, May I also live to see the land of Israel.

It's January 29, 1950. Rabbi Schwartz conducted a pidyon haben for Leonard's son. Mr. Northman was the Kohen. It was a very fine ceremony (with about 20 people), and we enjoyed it very much. May God give him a healthy manhood. Amen, Amen. Thank God for all.

It's January 30, 1950. Leonard moved into his new house on Colony Street. May this be a fortunate hour.

Now, please God, help Leonard earn a living for himself and his family. And allow him and his family to give us joy.

It took Leonard 4 months to build his house. Now, God should help him to pay it off. Amen, Amen. Thank God for everything. If one lives long enough, one will eventually see good.

Esther and I gave Leonard $34 for three lamps. May he use them in good health. Also, the house is now being furnished, and it looks like he'll have a nice home.

It's February 4, 1950. On Sunday, we went to visit Leonard in his home. Everything looked in very good order. Ethel's parents were also there.

The boy is a very sweet and healthy child. May God see that he remains so.

In due time, the house will be completely furnished. Thank God for everything.

It's February 12, 1950. Esther and I went to Bridgeport for Ethel's brother's (Norman) wedding. Norman married Miss Ethel Fleisher. We wished him good luck and we enjoyed ourselves very much.

Leonard's child is very handsome and good, and may God give him good health.

We gave Leonard $325 to help him financially. One has to help. Praise God.

Samuel notes that Dr. Skluth opened an office in Norwalk. Herbert Skluth is a distant relative who specialized in the treatment of diabetes. Obviously, Samuel was pleased by this circumstance, and he attached the following newspaper clipping to his diary:

DR. L. H. SKLUTH TO PRACTICE HERE

Announcement was made today of the association of Dr. Herbert Skluth of New York City with the office of Dr. Edwin D. Flanagan, 141 West Avenue, in the practice of internal medicine.

Dr. Skluth is a 1936 graduate of the Bellevue Medical College of New York University and after serving his internship in Harlem Hospital became the resident physician of that institution. A diagnostician in internal medicine, cardiology and diabetes, he is a diplomate of the American Board of Internal Medicine and a member of the American Diabetic Society.

During the war, Dr. Skluth served as a major in the Medical Department of the U.S. Army in the Pacific Theatre of Operations where he was twice decorated with the Bronze Star with Oak Leaf Cluster.

With Mrs. Skluth and their daughter Myra, Dr. Skluth will soon take up residence in this city.

Shortly after mentioning Dr. Skluth, Samuel also indicates that "Mr. Harris left for Israel." This comment is followed by a Yiddish newspaper article that announced the first voyage of tourists to the state of Israel, on a ship named *La Guardia*. The article also provided a description of the trip, the reception planned in Israel, and a wish for a peaceful journey. Presumably, Mr. Harris was on the ship, and perhaps, given Samuel's previous commentary, he hopes to follow suit.

Samuel also mentions my (Paul Abramson's) *pidyon haben*, which literally means "the redemption of the son." This term is derived from the custom of setting aside the first of everything—fruit, cattle, male children—for the service of God. Originally, this custom required that firstborn males were expected to be priests for the Jewish people. However, when the priesthood became concentrated in the family of Aaron, the first-born were no longer expected to fulfill this role. Nonetheless, Judaism still continues to recognize the special status of the firstborn through a ceremony that "redeems" firstborn males from the obligation of priestly service. Finally, firstborn sons of the Kohanim (priests) and Leviim (Levites) families are not redeemed, because they retain ritual service obligations.

My *pidyon haben* ceremony was conducted in the presence of a Kohen (Mr. Northman) and invited guests. It was held on the 31st day after my birth, which signified that I was "fully viable." During this ceremony, my father presented me, perhaps on a specially embellished tray, to the Kohen. The Kohen, in turn, asked my father (in an ancient Aramaic formula) if he wished to redeem his son, or to leave him to the Kohen (priest). My father, in reply, expressed the desire to keep me, and as "redemption," handed the Kohen five silver *shekels* (or dollars). Afterwards, my father recited a benediction for the fulfillment of the commandment of redemption, and another for thanksgiving.

Eventually, the Kohen concluded (three times) that "your son is redeemed," and I was returned to my father. Last, the Kohen recited a benediction over a cup of wine, and pronounced a priestly blessing over me. A festive banquet followed.

Samuel also indicates that I was "very sweet and healthy," and "very handsome and good." Yet he refers to me as "Leonard's son", rather than "Paul," or "my grandson." In contrast, Judy was immediately "our grandchild." Perhaps Samuel was now cautious with his attachments.

Finally, Samuel also notes that, "We gave Leonard $325 to help him financially. One has to help." Unfortunately, Samuel's comments belie the fact that Leonard was working for Samuel without compensation. Thus, Samuel's "financial help" is misleading. If "one has to help," Samuel should have paid Leonard a just wage. Instead, perhaps this demonstrates Samuel's disregard for Leonard's independence and achievements. Furthermore, while Leonard certainly needed to be gainfully employed, Samuel's assistance seems manipulative, rather than munificent.

*   *   *

It's March 20, 1950. On Sunday, we went to New York to see a Jewish play, "Sadie is a Lady." It was at the Second Avenue Theatre, and it starred Molly Picon. Mr. Kenner had given us the tickets, and Mr. Yisels treated us to dinner. We had a good time.

Business is a bit better.

I bought Leonard a tallis. May he use it in good health.

It's March 23, 1950. Praise God, Mr. Harris returned, in peace, from Israel. He's very satisfied with his trip.

It's April 6, 1959. My mother stayed with us during the week of Pesach. She's having a good time. Also, Leonard and his wife came to the seder, as did Sylvia and her husband.

I went to Dr. Skluth for a check-up.

Business is a little better.

May we live, and be together again next year. Amen, Amen.

It's April 27, 1950. Leonard is having a great deal of trouble with the land (in Green Farms off River Oaks Road) he bought with Dr. Margold. My brother-in-law (Abe Slavitt) is making it very difficult for Leonard to complete the deal. Don't I suffer enough? Especially seeing my son having such a hard time? But God will help, and everything will work out. One has to learn to adapt to these times.

Business is a little weaker.

It's May 7, 1950. This Sunday, in the month of Iyar, Ruben Michaels passed away. He was a very good friend of mine and we got along very well. May he intercede in our behalf and bring us goodness in heaven. Amen.

It's June 25, 1950. The war in Korea has begun, and America has entered the battle.

It's July 15, 1950. Jerry Epstein made me move from my storeroom, where I kept my stock. He raised my rent to $20 a month. Instead, I will now pay Sitwan $10 a month. However, this is an annoyance because the new place is farther from my store. But I can't help it.

It's August 13, 1950. Mrs. Schnabel died suddenly Friday night. She was 83 years old. We went to the funeral, which was Sunday, in the month of Elul. May she rest in peace.

It's August 17, 1950. Leonard was in Bridgeport today. He's attempting to settle the deal with Dr. Margold, in which he purchased 37 acres of land. Unfortunately, he's had financial trouble with that transaction.

It's August 24, 1950. My beloved daughter Sylvia will be in the hospital for one week. She has to have an operation. May God return her to good health.

Sylvia was operated on, on Friday, August 25. Fortunately, she is feeling good, thank God. And she'll be coming home next week. Thank God for everything.

It's August 28, 1950. Sylvia feels good, thank God. However, today she called from the hospital and told us that she has to remain there for a few more days. Thank God for everything.

It's August 29, 1950. Today, Grandma Esther and her grandchild Paul went to Stamford to buy him a pair of shoes. May he wear them in good health. And may he be a source of much joy for us. Amen, Amen.

It's September l, 1950. Thank God, Sylvia came out of the hospital. May she continue to be well, and may we have much happiness from her. Thank God for all.

It's September 8, 1950. Today, the National Guard was sent to the Korean battlefront.

It's September 21, 1950. America has lost 5,000 soldiers in the Korean War. And now America and her allies are 3 miles from Manchuria. God help that the war will end soon.

It's October 8, 1950. We went to a party for Attorney and Mrs. Abe Slavitt. It was their 25th wedding anniversary. However, my son Leonard didn't attend. He's still having problems with Abe and Dr. Margold, but we hope he'll be able to resolve them.

In the meantime, we have now loaned him a total of $500 in cash. Also, he redeemed $775 in government bonds, the bonds we'd been saving for his daughter Judy. Unfortunately, his problems with Dr. Margold have now lasted 6 months.

It remains to be seen how this will he resolved. Let's hope for the best.

It's November 21, 1950. Congratulations. My Sylvia purchased a house, a five-room bungalow. May she use it in good health. The price was $15,400, and it's located at 33 Park Hill Road. At present, the rooms need to be painted.

Sylvia certainly earned this house. She is a devoted daughter, who has helped us in every way. May it be with Mazel.

Samuel mention's Sylvia's surgery and her recuperation. However, not surprisingly, the details are missing. The surgery, by the way, was implemented to remove an ovarian cyst.

I (Paul Abramson) would not describe Sylvia's house as a "five-room bungalow." It was a beautiful home, of individual design, and included arched teak ceilings. As mentioned above, it cost $15,400. In contrast, Samuel's home, purchased 6 years earlier, cost $7,000.

Samuel also mentions that Leonard was entangled in a business transaction with Dr. Margold. Family legend indicates that my father and Dr. Margold entered a real estate development partnership. Dr. Margold provided the capital, and my father was to provide the construction and development. However, the construction was slower than anticipated, and Dr. Margold wanted a quicker return on his investment. The additional conflict with Abraham Slavitt resulted from the fact that my uncle represented Dr. Margold.

This partnership was finally severed in 1954. At that time, my family was living on a 7-acre Colonial estate (with huge columns, six bedrooms, elevator, wine cellar, arboretum, and so on). My father was to develop the surrounding 6 acres, eventually gaining title to the home (and part of the profits). However, my father failed to get a zoning clearance for the additional land, and the ensuing lawsuit forced our family to move back to South Norwalk. Interestingly, the subsequent investors gained the zoning clearance and developed the land for substantial profits. Thus, like many of my father's entrepreneurial ideas, the failure was in the manner of implementation (or unconscious obstacles), not the soundness of the design.

Although Samuel implicates Abraham Slavitt, it did not diminish Samuel's interest in the anniversary party. Leonard, not surprisingly, failed to attend. The following newspaper article describes this occasion:

WED 25 YEARS

Atty. and Mrs. A. D. Slavitt Entertain in Honor of Occasion at the Longshore Club.

Atty. and Mrs. Abraham D. Slavitt of 141 East Avenue, whose silver wedding day occurred on Wednesday, were hosts Sunday night to a large gathering of relatives and friends at the Longshore Beach and Country Club Westport, for a buffet supper party and dance.

Ernie Harris' Orchestra provided music for the evening with Miss Marie Auleta, vocalist. A profusion of floral arrangements added much to the attractive setting.

Included among the guests were the mothers of the couple, Mrs. Robert Abramson of this city and Mrs. David Slavitt of Bridgeport.

Atty. and Mrs. Slavitt are well-known residents in the community. Mrs. Slavitt is the former Miss Jennie Abramson. Both have long been identified with local Jewish organizations. Atty. Slavitt is associated in the practice of law with Atty. Paul R. Connery in offices in Washington Street. The couple have two children, Robert, a law student at New York University, and Donna, a student at the Thomas School.

Finally, Samuel mentions that he bought a *tallis* for Leonard. Originally, *tallis* meant "gown" or "cloak," and was worn as such. Today however, *tallis* refers to a four-cornered garment that is called a prayer shawl. It is worn by Jewish males during the morning prayers and on *Yom Kippur*. Moreover, before putting a *tallis* on, the following blessing is recited: "Blessed art Thou, O Lord, Our God, King of the universe, Who hast sanctified us by Thy commandments, and hast commanded us to wrap ourselves in the fringed garment."

Was this Leonard's first *tallis*? In some communities, boys begin to wear a *tallis* after the *bar mitzvah*. However, in other communities, it is worn after marriage. Perhaps when Leonard went into the army, he didn't need a *tallis*, and by the time he finished, he was no longer married. Also, after getting married a second time, Leonard immediately moved to Houston. Conceivably, it wasn't until Leonard returned to Norwalk, that Samuel remembered (or acknowledged) this deficit.

EPILOGUE

November 21, 1950 was Samuel's last diary entry. Eight days later (December 4, 1950), he died of a massive heart attack, at 65 years of age. Strangely enough, 14 years later, on the same day, his wife Esther died (at 73 years of age).

Sylvia sufficiently recovered from her surgery to give birth to a daughter, her only child, in 1953. However, her postpartum was arduous, involving severe depression that was treated briefly by electroshock therapy. Worse yet, several years after her daughter's birth, Sylvia developed Parkinson's disease (which the *Merck Manual* defines as a chronic central nervous system disorder, characterized by slowness and poverty of purposeful movement, muscular rigidity, and tremor). This disease eventually proved incapacitating, which prompted Sylvia's physical and psychological withdrawal from her surroundings. Eventually, Sylvia was confined to a Jewish nursing home, where she died in 1990. Her husband Irving, who died in 1991, was known within family circles as a quiet and patient man who always stood at his wife's side.

Samuel's mother, Fannie (or "Vichna"), Abramson died on June 10, 1952 (at 86 years of age). Several years later, Samuel's cherished house on Cedar Street was demolished to make way for Interstate 95.

As mentioned earlier, Leonard Abramson died on February 2, 1975 (at 59 years of age). His life was marred by continuous financial and psychological crises. After his death, Ethel Abramson moved back to Bridgeport, Connecticut, the city of her birth. Eventually, Ethel reestablished herself as a nurse and married a retired (and widowed) businessman (Lou Levinson) from Bridgeport. Recently, on November 2, 1990, Lou Levinson also died.

Finally, I also located Judy Abramson. She is married and still living in Norwalk, Connecticut. We have talked twice. After our second conversation, I wrote the following letter:

Dear Judy, I want to first thank you for being so friendly and helpful. It was not an easy phone call for me to make and certainly could have been awkward. I appreciate your time and consideration in helping me learn about a part of my life that had previously been a secret.

As astounding as it may seem, my brothers, sister and I had no knowledge of your existence, or my father's previous marriage, until after he died (1975). Both my mother and father, and all of his relatives, conspired to hide the information. Moreover, we never came upon the information—even by chance—except the one time I mentioned to you . . .

I wrote that letter 8 years ago and, despite sending other letters and cards, have never heard from Judy again. Interestingly enough, Judy's teenage daughters know nothing about either my father or their grandmother's first marriage.

Samuel Abramson at the time
he immigrated from Russia.

Samuel Abramson in
New York.

Samuel Abramson as a
young man in America.

Samuel and Esther Abramson in Norwalk, Connecticut.

Sylvia Abramson as a
young girl.

SAMUEL ABRAMSON

DEALER IN

Groceries, Vegetables and Feed.

6 BOUTON STREET

SOUTH NORWALK, CONN.

TEL. 306

Samuel Abramson's grocery
store business card.

Samuel Abramson and his
daughter, Sylvia.

Samuel Abramson as a butcher.

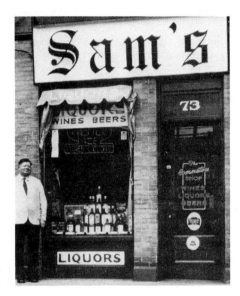

Samuel Abramson in
front of his liquor store.

A liquor label from Samuel Abramson's
Commuter's Liquor Shop.

Leonard Abramson (far right, top row)
as a boy scout.

Leonard Abramson in the Army.

Leonard Abramson (far right) with his friends
in the Army.

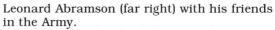

Ethel Esther Sakowitz Abramson as a nurse.

Samuel Abramson with his grandson Paul.

PART III

Case Study Methodology

And so this ends my grandfather's story, which was derived from his Yiddish diary, and enhanced with commentary and interpretations. What I will attempt to do now is to provide a more technical analysis of case study research. Although I will comment upon my grandfather's diary, this section will also provide a more general critique of case study methods. This critique is important because such methods are obviously not limited to the vagaries of my grandfather's diary, nor the manner in which it was handled.

This is a small book with two simple objectives. First, the book introduces an elaborate data set, the Yiddish diaries of a Russian Jewish immigrant. Second, this book also proposes two scientific rationales for case studies and attempts to illustrate how these rationales might be applicable in practice.

THE DATA

What contribution do these data (i.e. the diary) make? First, I believe they are unique. These data constitute a surviving diary, written in a relatively inaccessible language (i.e., handwritten Yiddish), of a man who died more than 40 years ago. Not coincidentally, that man was my grandfather.

Is Samuel Abramson, the person who emerges from the diary, also unique? On the one hand, certainly yes. He had the guts to leave home and family at 18 years of age. And when he arrived in the United States, he learned English, started a family, and experienced the trials and tribulations of economic independence. Finally, as an individual, he was an interesting blend of characteristics: Russian Jew, American immigrant, son, father, grandfather, volunteer police officer, peddler, gravedigger, tavern owner, folk artist, and so on. Undoubtedly, despite his many faults and worries, he was a special person with a variegated life. Certainly, my ability to write these words, as a UCLA psychology professor, owes no small favor to Samuel Abramson.

On the other hand, Samuel Abramson is also an "average Joe." His diary is not particularly eloquent, nor of much literary value (in contrast to the diaries by such authors as Stephen Spender, Alice James, and so on). Furthermore, he is one of many Russian Jewish immigrants who presumably shared similar experiences. Also, the economic instability and family "soap opera," are not unusual, given both the upheaval of emigration and the Jewish cultural context. Finally, Samuel started life in America as a factory worker and peddler, and ended life as a liquor store owner. Thus, he was neither extremely successful nor unsuccessful.

Regardless of Samuel Abramson's uniqueness, however, these data, in and of themselves, may have some value. For example, Samuel Abramson's generation of Russian Jewish immigrants is gone, which obviously limits personal testimonies from this population. Thus, such data may be important to understanding an extinct population with a unique historical record. This record includes escaping from Russia, the turmoil of transit to America, the confusion of entering America (e.g., Ellis Island, doctor's examinations, interrogation), and the problems of adapting to America (e.g., limited resources, a language barrier, discrimination, limited opportunities for employment, exploitation by employers and landlords, limited legal advocacy, limited medical services, and so forth).

Second, these data are also consistent with Runyan's (1982) criteria for an advantageous case study. Namely, Samuel Abramson's life history provides insight into his person in a realistic and vivid manner. Samuel comes alive, and his narrative represents at least one point on the graph of points that constitute the immigrant experience and assimilation into the United States.

THE THEORY

In Part I of this book I proposed conceptualizing Russian Jewish emigration (in the early twentieth century) as an investment that has a tremendous short-run downside risk, but a potential for long-term sustained growth. That is, although emigration was an expedient solution to problems at home, Russian Jews faced a plethora of obstacles in America, which in many ways offset the initial gains obtained by emigrating. However, as adaptation was achieved, and subsequent generations were produced, the substantial benefits of emigration were attained.

According to this perspective, Russian Jewish emigration was a long-term investment, whose gains operated according to a U-shaped curve, whereby initial obstacles diminished immediate rewards, but eventually, as a function of time, anticipated gains were produced. Thus, in many ways, the merit of the investment (i.e., emigration to America) was always viable, but the initial conditions were unstable, thereby delaying the eventual returns, which in this case were greater religious, financial, and educational possibilities in the United States.

Do the data presented herein support this proposition? On the surface, they appear to. For example, Samuel Abramson's immediate rewards for leaving Russia were quickly obfuscated by the trials and tribulations of his emigration, including transit to America, the disruption of family, the resultant poverty, a language barrier, discrimination, the absence of marketable skills, and so forth. Similarly, once Samuel established a financial foothold, conditions would change and adversity would prevail. Finally, these circumstances contributed to considerable psychological turmoil, which included depression, constant anxiety, and frequent obsessions.

Eventually, however, Samuel became a moderately successful small business person. However, his anxiety and obsessions remained strong. This is perhaps paradoxical, since he achieved financial stability, survived the Great Depression, was married to the same person for more than 40 years, provided opportunities for his children, and became integrated into a strong religious network. On the other hand, perhaps, as proposed, the disruption and turmoil of emigration (plus the factors that necessitated emigration in the first place) created insurmountable psychological obstacles, which no degree of stability or success could mitigate.

At least according to this theory, it should not be surprising to also discover that Samuel's son Leonard exhibited similar characteristics. Leonard failed to capitalize upon the educational and financial opportunities that presented themselves and, like his father, was plagued by a variety of psychological demons. Perhaps, as proposed, the ripple effect of the turmoil of emigration is not limited to the immigrant, but extends to his/her children as well (i.e., the continuing downside of the investment). Certainly, the conditions surrounding Samuel's first years in America were not ideal, and their psychological impact was obviously adverse. Thus, it seems reasonable to propose that raising children in that kind of environment is not going to produce the most advantageous psychological characteristics.

On the other hand, by the third generation, some progress should be evident. Greater opportunities should prevail, and more stability should exist. Therefore, it is interesting to note that Leonard's three sons include a UCLA professor, a Ph.D. systems engineer, and an attorney. His daughter, the best athlete of the group, was a collegiate swimmer who founded and edits her own sports magazine. (Similarly, three of the children also married spouses with professional degrees—psychologist, nuclear engineer, and audiologist.) Finally, one would propose that the children of these marriages would have even greater opportunities, and would show more evidence of psychological stability, thereby demonstrating that the substantial benefits (i.e., the long-term investment) of Samuel Abramson's emigration were obtained.

Now, although these data appear to support this proposition, how might this confirmation be falsified? First, the data (or interpretations made about the data) may be invalid, which would be a threat to the internal validity of this project. Second, while the data and interpretations may be correct, they may be relevant only to Samuel Abramson, which would be a threat to the external validity of this project. Finally, this project may include threats to both internal and external validity. That is, the data and interpretations may be invalid, and the findings (or theory) may not generalize to anyone.

Obviously, the threats to internal and external validity are reasonable concerns. For example, since the present case study relies upon a diary, several questions of validity arise. Is Samuel Abramson telling the truth? Or is he perpetuating a deliberate hoax? Not surprisingly, when we examined the diary, we were constantly looking for evidence that related to Samuel's honesty; the plausibility of his diary; and the integrity of his experiences (i.e., absence of contradictions, and so on).

However, even if Samuel did not intend to mislead the reader of his diary, inaccuracies are bound to be evident. Given that parts of this diary are retrospective, we must assume that the narrative entails forgetting, blending, personal biases, and factual distortion. And in that regard, when possible, we attempted to verify Samuel's facts against other documentary evidence, such as court proceedings, medical records, property deeds, and so on.

Of course, the most serious concern with Samuel's diary (and the data) is not the extent to which he intentionally distorted facts, but the extent to which he unintentionally colored his memory. A diary, by its very nature, is a subjective document. It is the writer's personal view of reality. Thus, we have attempted to suggest Samuel's biases and defenses (and highlight our own biases and defenses) in order to better gauge the value of this diary. Certainly, the ultimate utility of these data, as a contribution to theory and the archive of social science, depends upon their honesty, and perhaps psychological elaboration.

Of course, the diary has other problems. For example, we have no way of accurately gauging how normative Samuel's experiences were. In fact, it is probably better to presume the opposite, that is, that the diary is not representative of Jewish immigrant experiences. Thus, proceeding cautiously, perhaps we should conclude that the diary is an introspective document focused upon one person that, if we are lucky, has some relevance to the broad sets of data utilized in formulations about Russian Jewish immigrants.

In summation, this project may be falsified in a number of ways. First, one could demonstrate that the data are invalid and unreliable. Second, one could demonstrate that our elaborations are biased and unreliable. Third, one could demonstrate that these data are idiosyncratic, and can not be generalized to other Russian Jewish immigrants. Fourth, one could demonstrate that a different theory provides a better fit for these data (and other existing data). And so on.

Last, at the qualitative level, one must also question how valuable this data set is. The answer (independent of methodological issues) usually depends upon the reason for its creation. For example, an egotistical diary may be worthless. But a life story that highlights pathos, joy, vulnerability, and reflection may yield important and poignant insights. It can be the source of our intimate knowledge about people, and a humane and integrated approach to the study of a person, beyond the collection of test scores and cursory evaluations. And according to this perspective, the reader also has to determine if the present diary satisfies these criteria.

THE MERITS OF CASE STUDIES

Last, but not least, I will present my two rationales for case study research. This section comes at the end of this book because I believe that these data (the diary) are ultimately more important than my rationales. However, now that the data (and theory) have been presented and developed, I will introduce the rationales that were instrumental to the construction of this book.

When I received my grandfather's diaries, I was forced to evaluate what I wanted to do with them. I was, of course, toying with the prospect of using the diaries in a broader psychological analysis, perhaps as a case study, that is, a nonexperimental study of one person or event, with data

derived from long-term psychotherapy, protracted interviews, or extensive personal documents (Allport, 1942;
Runyan, 1982; Yin, 1989). I reasoned that if the diary
proved illuminating, I'd have a detailed record of a Russian Jew's adaptation to life in the United States, which, if
handled well, could be very instructive.

On the other hand, it was equally probable (or more
likely probable) that the diaries had no psychological
merit, except presumably to my family. More troubling,
however, was the question of whether there was any legiti-
mate rationale for pursuing the diary as an act of science
(or social science, for that matter). Clearly, by all conventional methods of science, the diaries could be nothing
more than diaries, replete with biases and obvious limitations in internal and external validity. Furthermore, since
the diaries were of personal interest to me, I was in no position to objectively evaluate their contribution. Therefore,
in addition to considering the merit or relevance of my
grandfather's diaries, I also sought a more basic question,
that is, what is the merit or relevance of a case study?

As mentioned above, I came up with two ideas. Paradoxically, these ideas are inconsistent with each other. However, since they both seemed reasonable, they are
included herein. The first one is titled "Adjunct to Induction," the second one (which, incidentally, I prefer) is titled
"Extrapolations from Popper's Philosophy of Science."

At this point I want to also address the distinction between single-case research designs and case studies. A
single-case research design is an experimental investigation with one subject (Kazdin, 1982). It often involves testable theory, for example, operant conditioning (Skinner,
1956), and utilizes experimental designs, such as in-
trasubject-replication (Sidman, 1960) and ABAB designs
(Kazdin, 1982), which facilitate verification of theory. Also,
the single-case research tradition is quite extensive (Davidson & Costello, 1969; Dukes, 1965; Hersen & Barlow,
1976; Kazdin, 1982; Robinson & Foster, 1979), and addresses many of the factors jeopardizing internal and external validity in experimental or quasi-experimental
designs (Campbell & Stanley, 1963; Cook & Campbell,

1979). Consequently, it is quite different from a case study (i.e., a nonexperimental investigation of one person, which often uses archival material), and in fact, single-case research designs were introduced as a means of overcoming the deficits of case studies, without discarding research on one (or a few) subjects.

ADJUNCT TO INDUCTION

What is the enterprise of science? According to Einstein (1953), science starts with facts and ends with facts, no matter what theoretical structures are built in between. Accordingly, the scientific method is often presumed (in the Baconian tradition) to proceed in a cyclic manner, whereby the scientist inductively organizes observations (or facts) into a theory. (In the physical sciences, the theory is formulated mathematically, which facilitates the explicit implications of the model.) Next, the scientist is presumed to deduce predictions from the theory, which are verified either experimentally or through observation. If the new facts are consistent with the predictions, the theory is retained. However, if the facts are contrary to the theory, the initial theory is abandoned in favor of a theory that better fits the facts. Finally, although it may appear that experiments verify theories, this assumption is not quite correct. Experiments (or observations) verify logical consequences (or predictions) of the theory. Theories, in the absolute sense, are usually incapable of verification. Instead, hypotheses derived from the theory are more amenable to experimentation or observation (Kemeny, 1959).

Although this is the traditional metaphor for the process of science, there are certainly other perspectives. Popper (1972, 1983), for one, considers induction to be a fiction and deems the method of science to rely solely upon criticism. Alternatively, Kuhn (1962), believes that scientific revolutions constitute shifting paradigms, or fundamental inventions of a new paradigm, which do not necessarily follow the programmatic scheme of traditional science.

These exceptions notwithstanding, for the purpose of the present rationale, traditional science will be retained as the benchmark for evaluation. However, before elaborating upon this method of science, it might be useful to question at this point where in the cycle might a case study fit. For example, a case study (e.g., the interpretation of a diary) is certainly not a theory. It does not explain facts (diaries are not necessarily facts), nor does it necessarily generate verifiable predictions. Also, it is quite difficult to conceive of formulating a case study within a mathematical language. This is obviously a serious problem, especially from a traditional science perspective, because mathematical theories are considered advantageous, due to their explicit implications, wide applicability, and consensual meaning. While this stringent definition of theory is certainly relaxed within the social sciences, it is important, at least for the present time, to scrutinize case studies against the more rigorous standards.

Perhaps a case study could serve as an experiment, or observation, in which facts predicted by a theory are verified? If we exclude, for the moment, issues relevant to design and measurement (e.g., internal and external validity), it seems reasonable to propose that case study data (interviews, diaries, and so on) are amenable for checking facts against theories (certainly as suggested by the example used in this book). Similarly, a case study might facilitate the process of induction. That is, at least hypothetically, facts from a case study might facilitate the development of a theory.

Unfortunately, as an experiment, although exceptions certainly exist (see Yin, 1989), the case study is often untenable for a variety of reasons, including problematic theories, experimental confounds, and faulty measurement. Another problem with conceptualizing the case study as an experiment is the issue of prediction. In the field of personality (e.g., Freud), it was often presumed that the case study was a viable method for testing theory (e.g., psychoanalysis) in addition to facilitating broader predictions about human behavior. However, as discussed above, the case study is, at best, a very limited experiment, and where prediction is concerned, it is often problematic. This latter issue, as it applies more generally to clinical methods, has been carefully examined by Paul Meehl and his colleagues (Meehl, 1954; 1973; Dawes, Faust & Meehl, 1988).

In the context of good science (at least the traditional perspective that utilizes explicit theories to fully describe and predict facts, employs sound measurement devices, and so on), a well-established theory could facilitate the prediction of nonintuitive, or counterintuitive findings, which might be difficult to predict statistically. However, where the social sciences are concerned, this advantage is obviously compromised by obtuse theories and questionable measurement devices. Therefore, if a rationale exists for the use of case studies for "theory generated predictions" in the social sciences, perhaps it involves the recognition of rare events (e.g., the "revelatory case," as described by Yin, 1989). Meehl (1954) has referred to this circumstance as the "broken leg" problem. For example, although an actuarial formula may be highly successful in predicting an individual's jogging behavior, it should be discarded upon discovering that the individual has a broken leg. In this regard, the case study researcher (e.g., clinical psychologist) may be able to improve upon the actuarial method if she or he can either recognize or detect rare/atypical facts/individuals.

While this seems to be a reasonable idea, a word of caution is advised. When examined experimentally, the potential benefit of detecting atypical cases is offset by the tendency to identify many cases as "rare," which, paradoxically, is inconsistent with the definition. That is, in practice, clinical judgment fails to capitalize on rare events because it claims so many events as rare (i.e., a large number of false positives) (Dawes et al, 1988). This problem is obviously complicated by the measurement strategy used to identify rare events.

Another problem with case studies also exists. For example, it is often stated that making measurements is the fundamental activity in which a scientist engages. Consequently, it is presumed that without measurements, scientific progress is impossible (Kemeny, 1959). If true, these pronouncements certainly question the legitimacy of case studies, especially as a form of experimentation. On the other hand, perhaps the credibility of case studies can be enhanced by including an additional form of measurement, such as a personality scale. This assumption, while plausible, requires closer scrutiny.

What makes a case study a weak experiment? First, case study data are often unreliable facts. And second, the absence of precise theory often undermines the utility of case study methods. Consequently, the critical question becomes: Can additional measurement, such as a personality scale, either enhance the objectivity of case study data, or provide a better theory?

In general, the answer is no. Since the majority of psychological tests do not satisfy the rigorous criteria for validity and reliability, they usually do not enhance the scientific legitimacy of a case study project, except perhaps to give it a different veneer. In fact, if psychological tests are used for additional interpretations, they could also compound the measurement error. To use a simple analogy, let us presume that I am trying to solve a murder mystery. I interview one unreliable witness, the butler, and he tells me that the maid did it. Similarly, I interview a second unreliable witness, the gardener, and he also tells me that the maid did it. Now, if both are unreliable, this consensus does little to help me discover the true murderer (in this case, the chauffeur). Furthermore, the unreliability could be counterproductive, especially if it gives me a false sense of confidence.

Therefore, it is quite easy to see that additional measurement, if not rigorously valid and reliable, does not facilitate the objectivity of case study data. Furthermore, such measurement obviously does not enhance theory. Thus, given the limitations of a case study as an experiment, it is probably better to avoid unnecessary "window-dressing," which may falsely inflate the scientific appearance of a case study. Instead, it is probably better to search for a more defendable rationale for a case study (i.e., besides being a theory or experiment) or for more rigorous methods that avoid unreliable measurement.

Where the later option is concerned, Katzner (1983) has introduced a variety of analytic procedures, which facilitate rigorous theoretical and empirical inquiry, yet do not rely upon quantification or measurement. Although Katzner notes that measurement is critical for standardization, distinction, and mathematical application, he also emphasizes that most important social variables are exceedingly difficult, if not impossible, to measure. As an alternative, Katzner suggests that, instead, we focus upon articulating the relationship between entities, using mathematical models, which avoid quantification. In this regard, the mathematical systems can yield viable laws, theories, predictions, and so forth, without regard to the capability of measurement. However, whether this approach has any relevance to a case study is more difficult to conceive. Generally, Katzner's focus is designed to provide mathematical models that systematize the relationship between parameters.

Consequently, using the traditional science perspective, we are faced with one last option: Case study data might facilitate the process of induction, or, more specifically, the development of a theory. Now, if we uphold our original definition of science, and reemphasize the necessity of facts, case study data fall short of this mark. Data derived from psychotherapy, personal documents, or interviews are subject to a variety of biases (e.g., distortion, and so on), that distinguish such data from fact. Furthermore, to argue that other forms of psychological data are similarly distorted does little to enhance our position. One might simply note that "two wrongs do not make a right." Therefore, if we are to persist with this option, we must first examine the rationale for relaxing the requirement for inductive facts. If such a rationale exists, we can then reconsider the relevance of case study data. Otherwise, we might as well "pack up and go home," because in the traditional cycle of science, it appears that case studies are neither facts, nor theories, nor experiments.

I believe that at least two conditions argue for the relaxation of inductive "facts." They are (a) the vagaries of the process of induction, and (b) probability theory, especially the theory of errors. Furthermore, I also believe that these conditions represent a reasonable rationale for case study data. Finally, I also believe that the problems inherent in case study data derive not from the absence of a reasonable rationale, but from misrepresentation, specifically in the form of conceptualizing case studies as facts, theories, or traditional experiments. The remainder of this section will address each of these issues.

According to the traditional science metaphor, the process by which a scientist forms a theory to explain observed facts is known as induction. Generally, induction is divided into the following two steps: (a) the formation of possible theories, and (b) the selection of one of these (Kemeny, 1959). Additionally, theoretical induction is also presumed to involve a mechanism beyond simply generating hypotheses to explain known facts. For example, if facts can be represented as points on a piece of graph paper, a curve that connects the facts can suffice as a hypothesis (i.e., an interpreted mathematical proposition that can be considered a possible theory). However, the conception of a significant theory is obviously something more than connecting the facts, since on the surface the facts (to most of us) appear unrelated (e.g., the motion of the moon and the falling of an apple).

Interestingly, Bertrand Russell (1948) believed that there is a principle that clearly justifies the scientific use of induction. According to Russell, induction assigns a probability to inferences derived from known facts, to occurrences that are beyond experience. That is, if a person is to know anything beyond his/her experience, there must be a law that permits him/her to make inferences from matters of fact. Such a law would be synthetic (i.e., not proved true by its falsehood being self-contradictory) and unlike the principles of deductive logic. Moreover, without such a law, complete skepticism would exist for all inferences, scientific or otherwise.

Similarly, Russell contended that all personal experiences and sensations represent "data," and that these data are always more valid than beliefs derived from them. Furthermore, Russell suggested that such data are the indispensable minimum of premises for our knowledge of matters of fact. However, Russell indicated that he is not contending that such data are always certain, but instead, that such data are important in the theory of knowledge.

Conversely, Russell also noted that these data can be misinterpreted. Thus, if data drawn from personal experience (e.g., "birds fly") can be misinterpreted (e.g., "all birds fly"), what relevance do they ultimately have to the enterprise of science? Russell, in response to this concern, suggested that such data give us an initial store of scientific laws, which, though often unreliable, facilitate the first steps toward science. And in this regard, perhaps a similar argument can be made for case study data, especially if they have relevance to at least one aspect of the scientific process (e.g., induction).

However, before evaluating this proposition more carefully, a broader question will be introduced. Why not consider every input (e.g., experience, books, films, conversations, and so on) relevant to incipient scientific laws? For example, why not consider the novels by Fydor Dostoyevsky essential to a theory of paranoia? Or the novels of Charles Bukowski essential to a theory of alcohol abuse? Certainly these books provide enormous insight and provoke considerable reflection. Therefore, why not consider them (or other such input) instrumental to the inductive side of the scientific enterprise?

Obviously, the biggest problem with relaxing the definition of fact, or relaxing the requirement for inductive facts, is the floodgate phenomenon. Open the gates, and all kinds of things will flow through under the guise of science. Perhaps, where case study data are concerned, it is advisable to paraphrase Russell's (1948) perspective as follows: (a) rely only on personal data, (b) presume these data are not always valid or reliable, and (c) view all interpretations drawn from these data with suspicion.

For example, in the case of a multiple personality, it might be helpful to document that such a condition exists. That is, one could present the personal testimony of a client that details a multiple personality. In the course of presenting this material, one could describe the context in which it was obtained, what cues may have prompted the dialogue, where distortions may occur, and so forth. Furthermore, if one avoided interpretations (e.g., this is obviously a consequence of sexual abuse), or misrepresentations (e.g., this case study clearly supports psychoanalytic theory), this material could suffice as data, albeit elaborate data, on the continuum of personality processes. And in this regard, these data may have some benefit. For instance: (a) They could be used inductively in a theory of personality formation (e.g., multiple personalities appear to exist); (b) since this is a rare occurrence, these data may have relevance to clinical prediction (i.e., Meehl's suggestion); and (c) using probability theory (either frequency or credibility), if someone is going to make a conjecture about a personality outcome, one needs to know the number of possible outcomes. Thus, data indicating that multiple personalities exist could facilitate that task.

Some additional basic notions about probability theory will also be considered. For example, where psychology is concerned, it is evident that most of what we study does not conform to inexorable laws. Thus, we tend to view the occurrence of behavior according to some form of probability (e.g., statistical frequency, credibility, and so on). Statistical probability is generally considered to be the relative frequency with which an event occurs in a certain class of events. Reichenbach (1953), for example, indicates that all probability statements can be analyzed in terms of frequencies. However, a number of authors (Carnap, 1950, 1953; Russell, 1948) have extended probability to include beliefs, credibility, or inductive probability, which is more consistent with informal usage, that is, given the available evidence, what are the chances something is true (e.g., it will rain tomorrow)?

In either case, probability theory usually presumes, at the very least, information on potential outcomes, such as heads/tails and the like. For example, if I am going to predict the gender of my next child, I will presume that the outcomes (male/female) will have equal probabilities. This conclusion also incorporates the principle of indifference, which assumes that the evidence related to this prediction does not contain anything that would favor one outcome over another. However, if my wife told me that she adhered to a special "miracle" diet, which greatly increased the chance of a female child, and if I discovered that this diet was effective, my prediction would obviously change as a consequence of my new evidence. Thus, recent mathematicians (e.g. Carnap, 1950, 1953) have suggested that inductive probability (or credibility) depends upon the observer and the evidence in his/her possession. And more specifically, Carnap believes that such inductive probability can be formalized, using logical analysis and mathematical calculation, into a tool for evaluating evidence in relation to a hypothesis.

In both examples cited above, the objective was to develop a valid theory (on gender outcome) in the form of a probability statement. Thus, knowledge of outcomes and additional evidence were essential inputs for the development of specific hypotheses. Now, to extend this conclusion more broadly, let us question whether case study data can enhance predictions by either articulating outcomes or providing additional evidence.

The two following issues will be addressed: (a) case study data that describe a frequent occurrence, and (b) case study data that describe an infrequent occurrence. Where a frequent occurrence is concerned, experience suggests that, other things being equal, an outcome is more probable than another if it has happened more frequently in the past. For example, if my car starts almost every day, I will presume tomorrow that my car will start. Although this perception can lead to certain fallacies (e.g., the Monte Carlo fallacy), in everyday life most things conform to this rule. Similarly, if a certain characteristic is predominant, and I'm going to make a blind selection, I will presume that my selection will be the dominant characteristic. Thus, in such cases, what can be gained by providing elaboration of a frequent or dominant occurrence, if this outcome is well known?

The crux of this question is, basically, what are the merits of case study data where the outcome is evident? That is, do case study data enhance theory development when alternative data (which may be more rigorous) exist? For example, if I have a statistical profile of the "average" college student (presumably drawn from a representative sample, using good measurement procedures), what can I gain from a case study of a college student? That is, what can I gain from a case, which may not be representative and probably utilizes data that are fraught with measurement error? Certainly, this question is significant, because it addresses the importance of case study data, independent of extenuating circumstances, such as atypical outcome.

Perhaps the most eloquent and provocative rationale for case study data exists in the writings of Runyan (1982, 1988). He notes at least seven advantages, which include:

1. Providing "insight" into the person, clarifying the previously meaningless or incomprehensible, suggesting previously unseen connections;
2. Providing a feel for the person, conveying the experience of having known or met him or her;
3. Helping us to understand the inner or subjective world of the person, how they think about their own experience, situation, problems, life;
4. Deepening our sympathy or empathy for the subject;
5. Effectively portraying the social and historical world that the person is living in;
6. Illuminating the causes (and meanings) of relevant events, experiences, and conditions; and
7. Being vivid, evocative, emotionally compelling to read (Runyan, 1982, p. 152).

Moreover, in addition to these advantages, Runyan also details a variety of methods that could enhance the presentation, reliability, and analysis of case study data.

Now, although these advantages are certainly open to debate, they are reasonable objectives when limited to input in the process of forming theories or hypotheses. Basically, these advantages suggest that case study data may be a rich source of information about a person. And as such, these data may enlarge the scope of knowledge about human lives (Pletsch, 1985). This does not, however, imply that such data are invariably valid or reliable, nor that inferences drawn from these data should be viewed without suspicion. It merely presumes that the formation of good theories represents "daring guesses on slender evidence" (Carnap, 1953), and consequently, case study data may enhance the evidence.

Second, case study data may be used to document an infrequent occurrence, or an atypical outcome, for example, the "revelatory case" (Yin, 1989). This objective, when applied to the formation of theories, has several advantages, especially in terms of providing additional evidence. For example, theories are presumably derived from facts, which are based upon experience and observation. If life experience, for average psychologists, is a continuous random variable, which is normally distributed, most of us have very similar experiences (within a couple of standard deviations). However, where the development of psychological theory is concerned, it might be instructive if we considered what can be gained by observing atypical outcomes (or "knowing your tail" in the bell shaped curve sense, as my colleague Keith Holyoak has remarked). Perhaps, as a first step, since such outcomes are rare (i.e., the far ends of the curve), they should be documented. Second, since they are beyond the experience of most psychologists (statistically, and by analogy, observationally), they should be expressed in greater detail, to facilitate observation. Finally, drawing upon Meehl's suggestion (Meehl, 1954; Dawes et al., 1988), atypical outcomes should be fully described to avoid confusion over what constitutes a rare event. Thus, to summarize, case study data derived from atypical cases have several distinct advantages as input to theory development. First, since such data are rare, they can help elucidate the upper and lower boundaries of experience. Second, such data can facilitate psychological prediction by documenting infrequent, non-obvious, or counterintuitive occurrences that may be missed by standard statistical (or empirical) approaches. And finally, atypical cases, or atypical data, are essential for understanding the range or variety of human experience, which is essential for understanding and appreciating the human condition.

What are the risks of suggesting this rationale for case study data? Perhaps one might argue that such data, or the pursuit of such data, will undermine either the credibility, or quantitative tradition of psychological research. Undoubtedly, this fear is augmented by 90 years of haphazard case studies (Hoaglin, Light, McPeek, Mosteller & Stoto, 1982). However, this concern is certainly overstated, especially when case study data are used judiciously. In the latter instance, such data can complement quantitative methods, without undermining a quantitative tradition (Yin, 1989).

In conclusion, I believe that a simple rationale exists for considering case study data as part of the enterprise of traditional science, in the form of inductive input. I also believe that this rationale has generally escaped recognition because psychologists have primarily used case studies to expound or test theories. As repeated above, case studies are usually neither facts, nor theories, nor experiments, and to represent them as such invites criticism and neglect. However, as input relevant to the formation of theories and hypotheses—either in terms of elaborating frequent or atypical outcomes—case study data can contribute in a meaningful way.

EXTRAPOLATIONS FROM POPPER'S PHILOSOPHY OF SCIENCE

I will now introduce a second rationale for case study research, which is based upon Popper's philosophy of science (1957, 1972, 1983). This rationale is quite simple, and is by no means original. Instead, it merely extends the application of falsifiability to case study research.

However, first, a word of caution. The preceding rationale is inconsistent with the present rationale. This was, perhaps, unavoidable. As the reader will note, the preceding rationale (induction) attempted to integrate case study research within the traditional Baconian metaphor of science. In contrast, the present rationale describes a different metaphor and examines case study research within this alternative perspective. Thus, since the perspectives are different, the rationales are, not surprisingly, inconsistent. Perhaps the induction rationale will appeal to those who endorse a traditional conception of science, whereas the second rationale will appeal to those who endorse Popper.

Popper (1983) contends that a theory has the status of belonging to the empirical sciences if and only if it is falsifiable. Second, Popper argues that the method of science consists primarily of rational criticism. That is, "scientific theories are distinguished from myths merely in being criticizable, and in being open to modification in the light of criticism" (Popper, 1983, p. 7). To Popper, there is no such thing as scientific method, let alone a preferred scientific method such as mathematics, or the methods of the physical sciences.

In this regard, Popper (1972) defines the aim of science to be the search for better and better explanations. Popper also contends that the explanation must be independently testable—and the greater the severity of the independent tests it has survived, the more satisfactory the explanation (Popper, 1957, 1972). Thus, in summation, according to Popper, good science means good explanation or theory. Furthermore, an explanation (or theory) is good if it can survive frequent and stringent examinations designed to falsify or refute it.

To extend this logic to case study research is quite simple. For example, since the scientific method now consists primarily of criticism, there is no justification for excluding case study research from the realm of science. Instead, case study research, like all research, is scientific, merely if the explanation it provides can be falsified. Furthermore, the propriety of the explanation is dependent upon its ability to survive rigorous attempts to falsify it.

The present case study was obviously written with Popper in mind. Data were introduced (i.e., the diaries) and a theory proposed (i.e., long-term investment) with the intent of providing a reasonable explanation of the psychological adaptation of a Russian Jew in early-twentieth-century America. At the same time, however, considerable attention was also directed toward threats to both the internal and the external validity inherent in this project.

It is hoped that the structure of this book captures the spirit of Popper's philosophy of science. Certainly, data were introduced and a theory was proposed, and the methods to refute (or falsify) these data and theory were delineated. More important, however, this book was written to facilitate the critical enterprise of science. That is, all conceivable biases and limitations were explicitly highlighted to expedite a thorough critique of this work.

CONCLUSION

To reiterate, this is a simple story about a simple man, my grandfather. In telling his story, through his diary, I have attempted to gain some insight into my grandfather, as well as into Russian Jews of his generation.

I have also attempted to conceptualize this work as case study research. In doing so, I have introduced a simple theory, examined the broader context of the diaries per se, discussed the relevance of personal documents for the social sciences, and explored two rationales for case study research.

Ultimately, however, this book is also a personal quest. Despite my being a psychologist, with a background in case studies (e.g., Abramson, 1984), this project was admittedly conceived (and doggedly pursued) because it was personally meaningful. I would not have undertaken this project—nor had the energy to sustain it for 5 years—if the data were not specific to my family. My interests lie elsewhere (e.g., sexual science), and despite appearances otherwise, these projects are inordinately difficult to complete. Thus, in conclusion, I think it accurate to conceptualize this book as serendipitous science, with very personal meaning. I hope, however, I have also surmounted these limitations, so as to make this book a broader contribution to the literature.

REFERENCES

Abramson, P. R. (1984). *Sarah: A sexual biography*. Albany: State University of New York Press.

Allport, G. W. (1942). *The use of personal documents in psychological science*. New York: Social Science Research Council.

Bailyn, B. (1982). The challenge of modern historiography. *American Historical Review, 87,* 1-24.

Barraclough, G. (1962). Scientific method and the work of the historian. In E. Nagel, P. Suppes, & A. Tarski (Eds.), *Logic, methodology and philosophy of science*. Palo Alto, CA: Stanford University Press.

Bein, A. (1941). *Theodore Herzl: A biography*. Philadelphia: The Jewish Publication Society of America.

Campbell, D. T., & Stanley, J. C. (1963). *Experimental and quasi-experimental designs for research*. Chicago: Rand McNally.

Carnap, R. (1950). *Logical foundations of probability*. Chicago: University of Chicago Press.

Carnap. R. (1953). What is probability? In D. M. Messick (Ed.), *Mathematical thinking in behavioral sciences*. San Francisco: Freeman.

Cook, T. D., & Campbell, D. T. (Eds.). (1979). *Quasi-experimentation: Design and analysis issues for field settings*. Chicago: Rand McNally.

Davidson, P. O., & Costello, C. G. (1969). *N=1. Experimental studies of single cases*. New York: Van Nostrand Reinhold.

Dawes, R. M., Faust, D., & Meehl, P. E. (1988). Clinical versus actuarial judgment. *Science, 243,* 1668-1674.

Dray, W. (1962). The historian's problem of selection. In E. Nagel, P. Suppes, & A. Tarski (Eds.), *Logic, methodology and philosophy of science*. Palo Alto, CA: Stanford University Press.

Dukes, W. F. (1965). N=1. *Psychological Bulletin, 64,* 74-79.

Einstein, A. (1953). The laws of science and the laws of ethics. In H. Feigl & M. Brodbeck (Eds.), *Readings in the philosophy of science*. New York: Appleton-Century-Crofts.

Hersen, M., & Barlow, D. H. (1976). *Single-case experimental designs: Strategies for studying behavior change*. New York: Pergamon.

195

Higham, J. (1983). *History: Professional scholarship in America.* Baltimore: Johns Hopkins University Press.

Hoaglin, D. C., Light, R. J., McPeek, B., Mosteller, F., & Stoto, M. A. (1982). *Data for decision: Information strategies for policymakers.* Cambridge, MA: Abt.

Kammen, M. (Ed.). (1980). *The past before us: Contemporary historical writing in the United States. Ithaca, NY: Cornell University Press.*

Katzner, D. W. (1983). *Analysis without measurement.* Cambridge: Cambridge University Press.

Kazdin, A. E. (1982). *Single-case research designs.* New York: Oxford University Press.

Kemeny, J. G. (1959). *A philosopher looks at science.* Princeton, NJ: D. Van Nostrand.

Kuhn, T. S. (1962). *The structure of scientific revolutions.* Chicago: University of Chicago Press.

Meehl, P. E. (1954). *Clinical versus statistical prediction.* Minneapolis: University of Minnesota Press.

Meehl, P. E. (1973). *Psychodiagnosis: Selected papers. Minneapolis: University of Minnesota Press.*

Pletsch, C. (1985). Subjectivity and biography. In S. H. Baron & C. Pletsch (Eds.), *Introspection in biography.* Hillsdale, NJ: Analytic Press.

Popper, K. (1957). *The poverty of historicism.* London: Ark.

Popper, K. (1972). *Objective knowledge.* Oxford, UK: Oxford University Press.

Popper, K. (1983). *Realism and the aim of science.* Totowa, NJ: Rowman & Littlefield.

Reichenbach, H. (1953). The logical foundations of the concept of probability. In H. Feigl & M. Brodbeck (Eds.), *Readings in the philosophy of science.* New York: Appleton-Century-Crofts.

Robinson, P. W., & Foster, D. F. (1979). *Experimental psychology: A small-n approach.* New York: Harper & Row.

Runyan, W. M. (1982). *Life histories and psychobiography.* New York: Oxford University Press.

Runyan, W. M. (1988). Reconceptualizing the relationships between history and psychology. In W. M. Runyan (Ed.), *Psychology and historical interpretation.* New York: Oxford University Press.

Russell, B. (1948). *Human knowledge: Its scope and limits.* New York: Simon & Schuster.

Sachar, A. L. (1967). *A history of the Jews.* New York: Knopf.

Sidman, M. (1960). *Tactics of scientific research.* New York: Basic books.

Skinner, B. F. (1956). A case history in scientific methods. *American Psychologist, 11,* 221-233.

Yin, R. K. (1989). *Case study research: Design and methods.* Newbury Park, CA: Sage.

ABOUT THE AUTHOR

Paul R. Abramson received his Ph.D. in Psychology from the University of Connecticut in 1976. Currently, he is a Professor of Psychology at UCLA and chair of the personality area. He is also editor of the *Journal of Sex Research*, and has served as a technical consultant to the Social Science Research Council, the United Nations, and the World Health Organization. Dr. Abramson's previous work in the area of case studies was the book *Sarah: A Sexual Biography*.